Crosspatch

INSPIRATIONS IN MULTI-BLOCK QUILTS

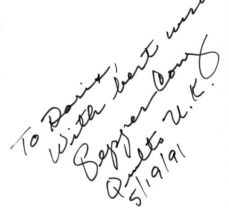

By Pepper Cory

C&T Publishing
Martinez, California

CROSSPATCH
INSPIRATIONS IN MULTI-BLOCK QUILTS
by Pepper Cory

Front Cover Photo:
The Time Travellers designed by Pepper Cory, pieced by Louise Mueller

Copyright © 1989 by Pepper Cory

Photography by Sharon Risedorph
San Francisco, CA

Edited by Nadene M. Hartley

Design & production coordination by Diana L. Grinwis
Grinwis Art Service, East Lansing, MI
This project was constructed on an IBM AT computer using Ventura 2.0 Professional Extension software.

Computer generated illustration by Jonathan Benallack
Windward Graphics, Lansing, MI
The illustrations were made on a MacIntosh Plus computer using Illustrator 88 software.

Cover calligraphy by Kathryn Darnell
Darnell Calligraphy & Illustration, East Lansing, Michigan

Published by
C&T Publishing
5021 Blum Rd. #1
Martinez, CA. 94553

ISBN 0-914881-26-4

Library of Congress Catalog Card No: 89-62339
Printed in the United States of America

TABLE OF CONTENTS

Foreword	1
Dedication	1
Acknowledgements	1
Introduction	3
Making This Book Work For You	4
Crosspatch—History and Definitions	5
Crosspatch Ancestors and Descendants	7
Choosing Blocks	15
Making Medallions in Crosspatch	23
The Quilts	25
Out of Bounds	44
Serendipity	46
Help in Making Crosspatch Quilts	49
Conclusion	55
Chart of Quilt Information	56
The Patterns	58
Bibliography and Supplies	67
About the Author	*Back cover*

FOREWORD

*T*his book evolved because I had an acute attack of hunger. Not a craving for cheesecake or chocolate lust, but rather I was hungry for knowledge. I had seen a quilt in a magazine that used two different blocks combined to make a beautiful overall design—a design more interesting than either one of the blocks separately. All of a sudden, I started asking questions: "How did the designer choose those particular blocks?" and "What guidelines are there in making quilts with more than one block?"

*C*ompelled by personal curiosity, I began to make my own two-block quilts. Some quilts grew to three-block designs. This book is the result of that experimentation. Like an explorer tracing a path in a new land, I have recorded my journey in multi-block quilts. And as the map-maker names new territories, I also have taken the liberty to name multi-block quilts. I call them Crosspatch quilts. Please use this book as you would a map, but feel free to wander off the path to explore your own Crosspatch quilts. Enjoy the journey!

DEDICATION

*T*his book is dedicated to my mother, Mary Elizabeth Wetzel Peddie, who is the most modern person I know. She adapts gracefully to change; unreservedly gives me her support, love, and encouragement; and realizes that, with the passing of time and the weathering of experience, even a late-bloomer can flower.

ACKNOWLEDGEMENTS

*Y*ou will notice a great many small, wall hanging-size quilts in this book. I allowed myself, for the first time in my quilting career, to lay aside my commitment to making full-size quilts and experimented in many ways by designing and making smaller quilts. The samples in this book would not have been completed, however, without the support and help of the following people, including: Judy Alwood, Norine Antuck, Colleen Beach, Bonnie Bus, Beth Donaldson, Marlene Eggert, Wanda Hansen, Connie Hartwick, Jeanette Hartwick, Gail Hill, Sherlee Mauch, Diana McGill, Terry McKenney-Person, Cindy Mielock, Louise Mueller, Nancy Myers, Mary Remmington, Carol and Bill Riffe, Carol Seamon, Judy Schimmel, Ann Snyder, Jill Stolpestad, Jeanette Thayer, and Cathy Thomas.

INTRODUCTION

The blocks in the quilts chosen for this book are easily constructed by hand or machine-piecing methods. They will not require advanced technical expertise, so the reader can concentrate on the fun and experimentation of learning.

The distinction between style, defined as color choice and placement, and method, how to chose blocks, can become blurred, especially since color carries great emotional weight. But the distinction between style and method is important, because, if you cannot choose compatible blocks, even a great color scheme will not entirely rescue the quilt. When a quilt looks "tricky" or when you cannot recognize the blocks, it is the style that hinders you from immediately breaking down the quilt into its component patterns.

One design, a combination of Ohio Star and Economy Patch (illustration 1), occurs in at least three different styles. It was a good, basic design used as I taught Crosspatch classes. You will see several students' variations of this design.

As you begin Crosspatch, here are a few guidelines to follow. One, please read the text and look at the how-to drawings. You will want to grasp both concepts of how to choose blocks and the style in which to design in order to understand Crosspatch. Two, practice looking at the quilts from the viewpoint of an artist. Try not to immediately jump to the game of picking out the patterns. Enjoy each quilt as a complete piece that, overall, presents a new design. Three, remember this book is only an outline of the possibilities when two or more blocks are combined in the same quilt. The more pieces you make, the better you will become at Crosspatch. The first quilt you make may not entirely satisfy you, but the second, third, and fourth will get progressively better. Keep exploring, keep changing the designs, keep working.

Illustration 1. The teaching study for Crosspatch classes.

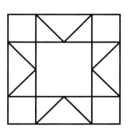

Ohio Star

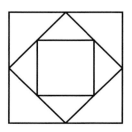

Economy Patch

MAKING THIS BOOK WORK FOR YOU

*H*ow exactly can you make Crosspatch work for you? Here are some suggestions.

*A*sk yourself what quilt in the book is your favorite. Study that quilt's photograph, examine the appropriate illustration, and read the chapter that explains that method. Begin designing a quilt for yourself that incorporates those blocks.

*I*f you are attracted by the designing process, but hesitant to cut fabric, turn to the **Personal Color Confidence Worksheet** (page 50). It's fun to take it with a friend, but don't collaborate. Each of you should write out your own answers, then discuss your differences and similarities.

*T*ake a piece of tracing paper and trace a graph of one of the quilts you like (or photocopy the graph). Do this four times. Using color pencils or felt-tip markers, color your graph four different ways.

*W*hen you're ready to cut cloth, select one of your really wild or unusual fabrics. Coordinate this fabric with one solid color, four small-scale prints, and a directional fabric such as a stripe, a plaid, or a check. Using these seven fabrics, pick a graph you like in the book and make that quilt in those fabrics.

*M*ake only the quilt top; don't worry about finishing it at this point. If you are not satisfied with your first attempt, make the piece again in those same fabrics but change the placement of the fabrics in the blocks. Resist the impulse to go back to your fabrics to make other choices. You will never know how good the piece might have been if you indulge in more decision making.

*I*f you need help in the technical aspects of patchwork construction or quilting, take time to review methods before getting started on a Crosspatch quilt. There are many good books that can help you. Some of these are listed in the Bibliography (page 67).

*W*hen you want to start Crosspatch, but feel temporarily immobilized because there seem to be too many choices, pick two quilts in the book that attract you. Mentally assign one quilt "heads" and the other "tails". Toss a coin and start with the winner. Beginning is the most important step!

The first time you read Crosspatch and before you attempt a quilt, sleep on it. Let the photographs, text, and illustrations percolate overnight in your brain. Navajo weavers often use this device to focus their creative energies before they begin weaving a rug. Sweet, colorful dreams!

A more complete definition of Crosspatch is needed before exploring this type of quilt. Crosspatch does not mean quilts that alternate pieced or appliqué blocks with plain squares. These quilts serve other purposes such as stretching the patchwork blocks to the requisite number for a quilt and allowing the quilter to show off her quilting stitches in the plain squares.

Crosspatch also does not mean the sampler type of quilt. Samplers are composed of a variety of quilt blocks. Historically, samplers were often made by a group of friends who each made a block at home, then together would assemble the top and

quilt the sampler for a special individual or an event (like a young woman leaving her friends to move west with her husband). These samplers were a harmonious compromise for the variable levels of skill of the quiltmakers. A new quilter could make a simple block, while a more experienced quilter would construct a more complex patch. The purpose of the sampler was to accommodate the talents of its makers while producing a collection of mementos that would be cherished by the recipient of the quilt. Nowadays samplers are usually made for a different purpose since constructing a sampler quilt is the most common form of instruction used in the

teaching of quilting. The modern sampler quilt is a novice quilter's "primer" and represents the "homework" for her first lessons in the craft. Crosspatch serves neither of these purposes.

Some patterns may seem to be categorized as two-block quilts, while in actuality, the shapes in the blocks are the same, but the colors reverse and the blocks change orientation within the quilt. The Drunkard's Path is the best example of this designing method that old-time quilters loosely labelled a "Lend and Borrow quilt". Other examples, often pieced in only two colors, are Hearts and Gizzards and

Illustration 2. Examples of "Lend and Borrow" patterns.

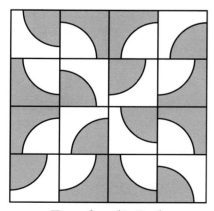

Drunkard's Path

World Without End

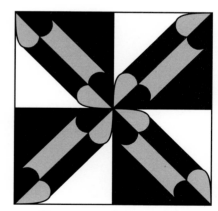

Hearts and Gizzards

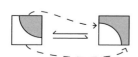

The basic block alternates colors and changes orientation within the quilt.

Illustration 3. "Square and Sash" patterns must combine a block with a pieced sashing to achieve an overall design.

Storm at Sea

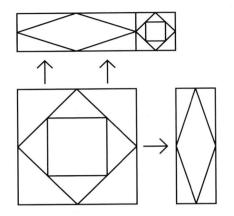

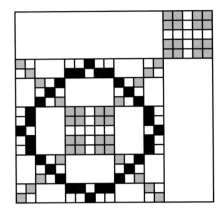

**Burgoyne's Quilt
(Burgoyne Surrounded)**

World Without End (illustration 2, photo 1).

*O*ne more traditional type of patchwork that is not Crosspatch is the Square and Sash blocks. These are quilts in which a block pattern is combined with a pieced sashing strip (sometimes called lattice) to achieve an overall design. Some of the most popular Square and Sash patterns are Burgoyne's Quilt (also called Burgoyne Surrounded) and Storm at Sea (illustration 3).

*S*o, if Crosspatch is *not* any of the following: blocks pieced with alternate plain squares, sampler quilts, Lend and Borrow quilts, or Square and Sash designs,

what is it? **Crosspatch quilts are those quilts in which different patterns are set side by side to produce new lines, movement, and visual interest when the quilt is viewed as a whole.**

*D*o you remember singing along with the "bouncing ball" to songs on the television? The bouncing ball directed the viewer to the timing of the words to be sung. Likewise when a traditional patchwork pattern is repeated in a quilt, our eyes bounce from block to block. We can, even by glimpsing the turned back corner of a traditional patchwork quilt, predict the whole design. But a Crosspatch quilt, whether it graces a wall or lays on the bed, is best viewed from a little distance, so that the beauty of the overall design can be appreciated.

*C*rosspatch quilts may be designed in many ways. They can even stretch the definition of what a quilt ought to look like, as the quilter goes "out-of-bounds" with her design. These are all possibilities for Crosspatch and the succeeding chapters will explain the design concepts more fully.

*B*ut before going on to new Crosspatch combinations, we need to take into account the only true groups of Crosspatch designs that are traditional patchwork. These two groups are the Irish Chains (of which there are many variations) and the Snowball patterns. These traditional Crosspatch designs are the bridge to any new Crosspatch combinations.

*T*he Irish Chain patterns have always been popular with American quiltmakers. Indeed, the Chain patterns also found favor with patchworkers in the British Isles and, consequently, represent some of our earliest patchwork patterns. While there are too many Irish Chain variations to list them all, a few that most quilters will recognize are the Single Irish Chain, the ever popular Double Irish Chain, and the Triple Irish Chain. A scrap version of the Double Irish Chain is called Jewelled Chain, and an interesting pattern with an Art Deco feeling is called Domino Chain or Dogwood Blossoms. These last two patterns are 20th-century variations and were probably popularized by the newspaper quilting columns of the 1920s and '30s. One Irish Chain variation that is almost exclusively found in Amish quilts is Railroad Crossing (illustration 4).

*O*ccasionally, at a quilt show or in an antique shop, you may find an Irish Chain quilt that is "just not right." The overall design seems off-center. This is a quilt that could have benefited from one more row of blocks to balance the pattern (illustration 5). If the quilt in question is an antique quilt, the quiltmaker could have run out of fabric or the bed for which the quilt was intended was only so big. It is an interesting phenomenon of quilters' reverence to tradition that we would spend time speculating on the motives of a long-gone quiltmaker.

Illustration 4. Some of the Irish Chain variations.

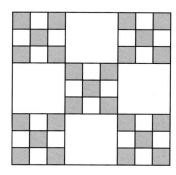

Single Irish Chain

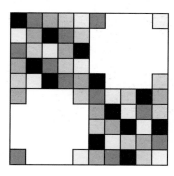

**Jeweled Chain
(a scrap pattern)**

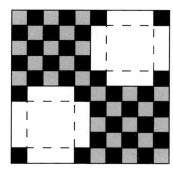

Double Irish Chain

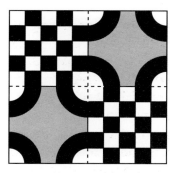

**Domino Chain
(Dogwood Blossoms)**

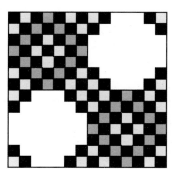

Triple Irish Chain

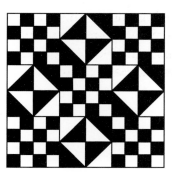

Railroad Crossing

Illustration 5. An antique Irish Chain quilt graph.

The block arrangement of this quilt looks unfinished. Notice that the four corners of the quilt are not all the same block. The quilt seems heavier on the left side in this four block across by five block down arrangement. An exact center of the quilt, difficult to discern, is on a seam, three blocks down and two blocks over, halfway up the block.

But if I saw a modern Irish Chain quilt that appeared off-center, I would be quick to criticize the maker's designing abilities. The quiltmaker of old and her present-day counterpart, however, probably shared the same liability. Neither comprehended that making a quilt that uses two different blocks requires a different planning approach than making a quilt with a single repeated block.

The lesson of the antique Irish Chain quilt is the basis for designing all balanced Crosspatch quilts. The four corner blocks of your Crosspatch should be the same pattern and there ought to be one center block to the quilt. In order to accomplish these requirements, remember the phrase **Odd By Odd.** This means your quilt should be an odd number of blocks across by an odd number of blocks down. The smallest number of Odd By Odd is three by three blocks, as in a nine block arrangement. When designing with two patterns in a nine block set, one of the patterns will be repeated five times and the other pattern four times. Remembering Odd By Odd, a balanced Crosspatch would be three by three blocks, five by five, five by seven and so on. With an Odd By Odd set, your quilt is assured of having four identical corners and a central block. Look at the graph of the antique Irish Chain quilt. Compare it to any of the balanced sets of the next drawing (illustration 6).

The Irish Chains break down into two basic blocks—a checkerboard and a plain block with

Illustration 6.
**ODD BY ODD sets ensure that the four corners of the quilt will be the
same block and that there will be a center block to the quilt.**

3 blocks across by 3 blocks down (*9 blocks total*)

5 blocks across by 5 blocks down (*25 blocks total*)

3 blocks across by 5 blocks down (*15 blocks total*)

5 blocks across by 7 blocks down (*35 blocks total*)

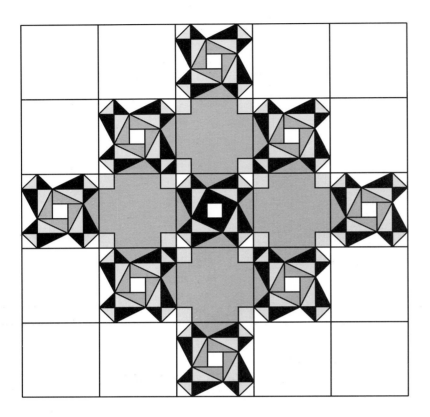

Illustration 7.
The *Galaxy* quilt is five blocks across by five blocks down. It includes three different patterns—Eccentric Star, Double Irish Chain, and a plain block.

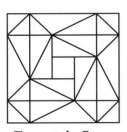

Eccentric Star

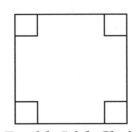

Double Irish Chain

Plain block

smaller blocks in the corners. When separating the Irish Chain blocks, the plain block seems to offer the most opportunities for combining well with other patterns. The Double Irish Chains belong to the five-patch group of patterns. Other five-patch patterns are obvious matches. An unusual pattern in the five-patch family called Eccentric Star is one such block. Arranging blocks in a five by five outline, I used the simple square of Double Irish Chain, Eccentric Star, and plain blocks. The result was a quilt I called *Galaxy* (illustration 7, photo 2). The illusion of curves is evident where the long triangles of Eccentric Star and the perpendicular lines of the corner squares of the Irish Chain meet. The large open spaces of the Irish Chain blocks and the plain squares also offer the opportunity to showcase a large, painterly print and elaborate handquilting.

*D*epending on the source consulted, the Triple Irish Chain is sometimes a five-patch, at other times a seven-patch block (illustration 8). The consistent feature that makes it a Triple Chain seems to be that there are at least three small blocks (occasionally more) in each corner of the simpler square.

*W*hen another five-patch pattern called Flying Squares is placed with a Triple Chain, the result is a very traditional-looking Chain variation (illustration 9, photo 3). The new Crosspatch was named *Dancing Chain*, since the Flying Squares reminded one of the figure of an exuberant dancer, one arm high over her head and the other straight out from

Illustration 8.

Depending on the source consulted, sometimes Triple Irish Chain is drawn as a seven-patch, other times as a five-patch. The seven-patch variation also has an alternate block. The factor that determines a Triple Chain seems to be that there are three, or more small squares in each corner of the simpler block.

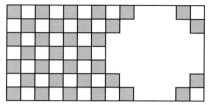

Triple Irish Chain (seven-patch)

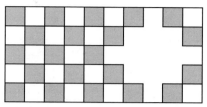

Triple Irish Chain (five-patch)

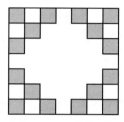

Alternate block

Illustration 9.
A new Chain pattern that was designed from a Triple Irish Chain (five-patch) and the Flying Squares block.

Dancing Chain

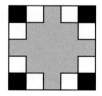

Irish Chain

Dancer

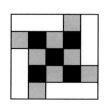

Flying Squares

Illustration 10.

A Crosspatch combination of Bear's Paw and Triple Irish Chain block A. This graph is for the *Sante Fe* wall hanging. Triple Irish Chain B is used in the *Ohio Amish Bear's Paw.*

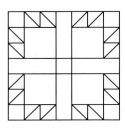

Bear's Paw

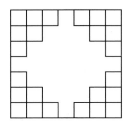

Triple Irish Chain A

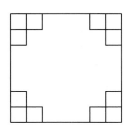

Triple Irish Chain B (alternate block)

the shoulder as she kicks out a leg and balances *en pointe* on the other. It seemed appropriate that the white marble-like fabric in the *Dancing Chain* sample was cut from hem scraps of a dancing dress owned by my friend, Betty.

*T*he other Triple Chain, from the seven-patch family, could combine with any number of interesting patterns. One popular seven-patch is Bear's Paw, which combined beautifully with two variations of Triple Chain to become twin wall hangings (illustration 10, photo 4). The first variation, *Santa Fe*, was pieced in southwestern colors (deep red, gold, turquoise, white, sky blue). It was made with the more elaborate Triple Chain block. The second variation in Bear's Paw and the simpler Triple Chain was pieced in colors reminiscent of Ohio Amish quilts (tobacco brown, black, beige, magenta, royal blue). Both wall hangings were constructed using strip piecing methods, but careful cutting with a rotary cutter; consistent measurement; and even, smooth machine stitching were necessary for the pieces to lie flat.

*I*n addition to the Irish Chains, the other traditional patterns that are true Crosspatch designs are the Snowball variations. These consist of a nine-patch checkerboard coupled with a square that has the corners knocked off, leaving an octagon. The three best-known versions are the antique Snowball, Tile Puzzle, and Around the Twist (illustration 11). Tile Puzzle and especially Around the Twist require careful color placement.

Illustration 11.
Some variations of the Snowball pattern.

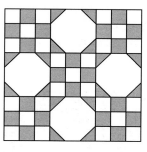

Antique Snowball

Nine Patch

Octagon Block

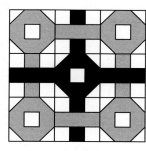

Tile Puzzle

Nine Patch Blocks

Octagon Blocks

Around the Twist

Nine Patch block changes orientation.

Octagon Blocks

**Illustration 12.
A Crosspatch combination of the Snowball
octagon and Water Wheel blocks for the wall
hangings *Portolani* and *Persian Fountains*.**

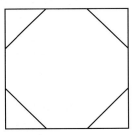

Snowball Octagon

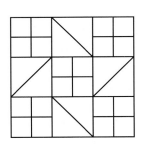

Water Wheel

*W*hen designing a Snowball variation, the octagon is the starting point. Another nine-patch pattern, such as Water Wheel, is a good choice as a companion block. The corner triangles of the octagon find continuation in the 45° lines of the Water Wheel points. Two wall hangings resulted from this Crosspatch (illustration 12, photo 6). One, called *Portolani*, has Water Wheel blocks pieced in black, blue, and brown prints, while the octagon blocks reveal an unusual map print. The term *portolani* means maps and was the term applied to the remnants of maps made by the ancient Greeks that pointed the way to the new world.

*T*he other wall hanging, pieced exactly the same as *Portolani*, is *Persian Fountains*. The unusual fabric in the octagons is four sections of a batik panel print.

*A*s you can see from the Irish Chain and Snowball hybrid examples, you can stay firmly rooted in traditional patchwork patterns as you invent new Crosspatch. There are so many possibilities using Chain and Snowball blocks that you may find it difficult to branch out into other Crosspatch designs. Before you whip out tracing paper and start any "back-to-the-future" research in Chain and Snowball quilts, please read on. There are even more interesting paths to explore.

CHOOSING BLOCKS

Illustration 13.
New areas of interest are possible when blocks are set side by side in Crosspatch quilts. More areas of interest means there are more design possibilities. Some new areas are highlighted.

*W*hen I was choosing blocks from which to make the sample quilts for this book, I used an elementary elimination process. I gathered every compendium, dictionary, guide, and collection of quilt patterns I owned, bought a pad of tracing paper, and sharpened my pencil. I made many drawings of quilt blocks. But after gathering these drawings of blocks, how did I decide what blocks combined would make good Crosspatch designs? My choices were guided only by my personal preference. But before you make the actual choices, here are points to keep in mind when approaching the design process.

*T*he first thing to think about before you start to make blocks is that the patterns chosen need not be complex, new, or different patterns. Indeed, considering simple traditional patterns such as a Nine Patch or Ohio Star as half of a Crosspatch combination makes good design sense. This is because Crosspatch more than doubles the effect of a single pattern since the quilt design has the first block, the second block, and then the new lines and patterns created where the blocks are tangent. Illustration 13 highlights several new areas of interest that result when Ohio Star and Economy Patch combine. When there are many areas of interest in a design, it means there are more possible choices for color placement. Good design is often simple design.

*H*ow many blocks should you consider for your first Crosspatch quilt? When you have selected the blocks to be combined, you will discover that just drawing one each of the blocks will not satisfy your designing desire. In most cases, nine blocks (three across by three down) is the least number of blocks to determine if the design can be successful. The nine-block sketches are called studies (illustration 14). Just as an artist makes many drawings before committing paint to canvas, so making studies will help you decide which pieces should make it into cloth. Crosspatch quilts may be constructed of a different number of blocks than nine, but as a designing tool, the study of nine blocks is where you need to begin. After you have chosen your blocks, draw a study. You may photocopy it several times and use the copies to exercise your colored pencils. When you are on a break at work, or you are a passenger on a long car trip, or you are stuck

Illustration 14.
A study in a drawing of nine blocks, the least number of blocks with to start designing Crosspatch combinations.

in bed with the flu, you'll find designing is the next best thing to quilting.

*I*f you looked up the word "compatible" in a dictionary, the definition might include the term "harmonious" or the phrase "capable of existing together." Quilters being rather eclectic, what is harmonious to one may be dull to another. These are not hard and fast rules for what block will look good with another block, but there are several guidelines that will make selecting compatible blocks easier.

Blocks With a Common Shape

*O*ne Crosspatch quilt design that works is the combination of Ohio Star and Economy Patch (illustration 1). The reason the design is successful is that both blocks have a prominent element in common, in this case, the squares at their centers. The principle for choice—that the blocks have a common shape within them—makes the blocks "echo" each other. The viewer finds them compatible because of the repeated elements. When you are looking for blocks, remember the idea of a repeated shape as a coordinating tool.

Cousins

*A*nother method of combining blocks is choosing "cousin" blocks. Most pattern reference books are arranged in chapters according to the basic structure of the blocks. In other words, patterns that break down into four-patch divisions are grouped together, patterns that are nine-patches are together and so on.

Start searching for compatible blocks within the same family of patterns. These "cousin" blocks are an obvious and easy method to use in combining patterns (illustration 15).

A step further in combining cousin blocks (second cousins?) might result in a study such as that in illustration 16 and photo 7. Here a nine-patch pattern, Shoo-Fly, is matched with a Kaleidoscope-type pattern. The shapes and lines within these two blocks are quite different. Shoo-Fly has squares and right triangles while the Kaleidoscope has wedge shapes. But these two can combine successfully because one of the blocks, the Kaleidoscope, is re-drafted to relate better to the Shoo-Fly. By drawing a plain square, with the tangent points of a nine-patch marked around the outside of the square, then connecting lines across the middle of the square dot-to-dot, New Kaleidoscope

Illustration 15.
A study for the quilts *Valentine's Boogy* and *Stormy Weather* (photo 6). These are cousin blocks.

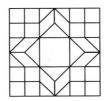

Aunt Sukey's Choice

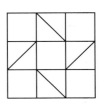

Wind Mill

Illustration 16. *Fourth of July* is a quilt which combines a Shoo-Fly block with a re-drafted version of Kaleidoscope.

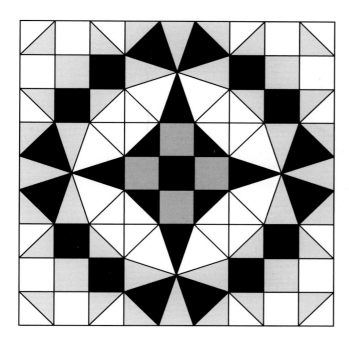

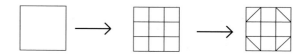

The Shoo-Fly is from the nine-patch family.

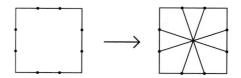

The second block is drawn by marking the tangent points of a Nine Patch, then drawing intersecting lines, dot-to-dot, across the block. The re-drafted block is New Kaleidoscope.

Illustration 17. Some X and O blocks.

X Blocks

King's Cross is an X block because of its construction.

Ohio Star is an X block here because of its color and fabric placement.

O Blocks

Economy Patch is an O block because it has a definite center.

Bachelor's Puzzle is an O block since all the movement in the block revolves around the center.

An X's and O's combination that is the study for Diana McGill's quilts in *Drought Series '88* (photo 8).

was formed. New Kaleidoscope has two different size wedges (unlike the traditional Kaleidoscope with one size wedge) and combines well with its companion, Shoo-Fly.

*T*his particular Crosspatch is intriguing since the casual viewer thinks the quilt design has curved lines. The illusion of a curve exists when a line of a particular angle meets, at a tangent point, another line of a different angle. The lines seem to intersect and curve. The "curve" is actually a series of variously angled lines. Our eyes tend to perceive the sum of the smaller straight lines as a curve, especially when we regard the study itself as a whole design, not merely nine separate blocks.

X's and O's

*P*erhaps you are a quiltmaker who would like to challenge yourself. Instead of Crosspatch combinations from similar sorts of blocks, you might try combining very different blocks in a quilt. One way to do this is by choosing **X** and **O** blocks. **X** blocks are patterns that either obviously by their construction resemble an X, or by virtue of their color placement, the blocks appear to have a diagonal feeling. **O** blocks, on the other **hand**, are patterns that have a definite center and are symmetrical in all directions (illustration 17). If you are excited by the concept of **X** and **O** Crosspatch, keep in mind a Tic-Tac-Toe gameboard as you choose blocks.

*T*he methods discussed so far for choosing blocks are based on the construction of the patterns. The following motivations for combining blocks are not technical but rather are guided by the individual creativity and preferences of the designer. These methods may also break out of the first one block, then a different block rhythm. The sets of these quilts may include only an occasional different block or they may feature blocks grouped together according to their pat-

---

Illustration 18. The graph for Shaylah Thornton's quilt.

The blocks, Next Door Neighbor and Friendship Star, were chosen to express affection for Shaylah and regret that she would be leaving our community. This quilt is an example of combining blocks for sentimental reasons.

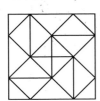

Next Door Neighbor

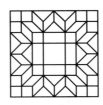

Friendship Star

18

tern while bordered by a line of blocks of another pattern.

Sentimental Reasons

You may also combine blocks for personal reasons. Perhaps the blocks Bachelor's Puzzle and Steps to the Altar seem appropriate as a Crosspatch quilt for a friend getting married. You may want to make a Crosspatch quilt for a friend who is moving. The Capitol City Quilt Guild of Lansing, Michigan, made such a quilt for their first president, Shaylah Thornton, when she moved from Michigan to California. Friendship Star combined with Next Door Neighbor for a stunning quilt. While Friendship Star was a complex block that the experienced piecers relished, Next Door Neighbor was a simple block that even the novice quiltmakers could piece. In this quilt, Crosspatch served a double purpose. The two patterns united in an exciting design, and all of Shaylah's friends, regardless of their expertise level, could participate (illustration 18, photo 9).

Crosspatch in Scrap Quilts

Scrap quilts have always been popular with quilters. Although the ostensible motive for making scrap quilts is to use up small or odd bits of fabric, the real attraction is that "scrapping" offers the opportunity for the quilter to experiment with new colors and patterns. The basic idea of Crosspatch—more than one quilt pattern—can be applied to scrap quilts. Often scrap quilts are made in very simple patterns, such as a Nine Patch. Another different block can be used to break up the symmetry of the scrap quilt and to draw attention to accent colors.

One such scrap quilt is in illustration 19, photo 10. Made by Marlene Eggert in 1987, this quilt effectively uses a second block, in this case Broken Dishes, to occasionally interrupt the predominately blue Nine Patch blocks. The Broken Dishes blocks "let the light in" and are the accent that flavors the whole piece into a harmonious—but not predictable—quilt.

Another version of Crosspatch in a scrap quilt is the calendar quilt approach. For a period of time, in the autumn of 1987, I made a block every day. I

Illustration 19.

This is the plan that Marlene Eggert followed as she pieced her scrap quilt (photo 10). The Nine Patch was the basic block but the Broken Dishes block was used to introduce light colored fabrics and to break up the predictable rhythm of the quilt.

Nine Patch

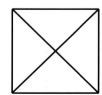

Broken Dishes

Illustration 20.

The plan for the *Calendar Quilt*, begun the first day of autumn, 1987. The Four Patch block was pieced Monday through Saturday and the Puss in the Corner was made for Sundays.

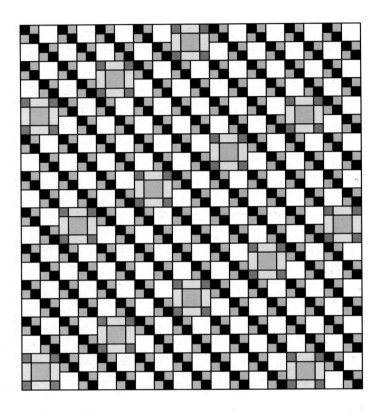

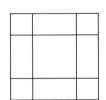

Puss in the Corner

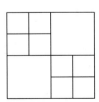

Four Patch

travelled and taught a lot that season and the methodical hand-piecing of a block became a daily ritual. Monday through Saturday I pieced Double Four Patches but on Sunday, I made a Puss in the Corner block. I collected the fabrics from people that I met. Often I recorded, in indelible marker, the dates on the blocks and sometimes a sentence or two about what I had done that day (illustration 20, photo 11). The quilt became both a fabric calendar and diary. The calendar approach could be even further expanded if you chose a different pattern for each day of the week.

The only directive to keep in mind, if you are doing a scrap Crosspatch, is to choose very simple blocks. The multitude of fabrics will naturally give the piece pizazz.

Artistic Intent

Perhaps you are taking an artistic, looser approach to designing your quilts. You may have an overriding desire to illustrate some larger artistic concept in your pieces, such as showing movement or conveying a particular emotion or memory. In that case, combining different quilt blocks in the same quilt is only a means to that end. I designed two quilts in this manner. In both cases, I chose colors and fabrics by the scenario method described in the **Personal Color Confidence Worksheet** (page 50).

*T*he quilt *Stroll in the Garden* was designed to carry the viewer's attention from upper right to lower left. The Rolling Stone blocks made a stair-step path in white, grey, and green. The "path" is bordered by Crosspatch blocks, their illusion of curves contrasting with the angularity of the path. Variable Star blocks in darker colors are reminiscent of the crossed timbers of a rail fence (illustration 21, photo 12).

*H*ave you ever looked up at the stars in a night sky and pondered, "I wonder if anyone is out there?" This dreamer's question is the source of inspiration for *The Time Travellers* (illustration 22, photo 13, on the cover). I had already been fooling with the three cousin blocks—Shoo-Fly, 54-40 or Fight, and Air Castle Star. The rotating star points of Air Castle Star seemed to suggest motion, so a central group of blocks of this pattern became the "travellers". The spikey, more dangerous-looking star points of 54-40 or Fight blocks made for a defensive ring around the travellers. A 54-40 or Fight star block as the point man (upper right corner) and again as the rear guard (lower left) reinforce this protective posture. The Shoo Fly

Illustration 21.

The graph for the quilt *Stroll in the Garden*. The purpose of the quilt is to illustrate movement. The Rolling Stone blocks make up the garden path; the Crosspatch blocks contrast with the geometric lines of the path; the Variable Star blocks border the quilt like a rail fence.

Rolling Stone

Variable Star

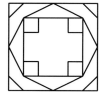

Crosspatch
(the name of this block pattern)

Illustration 22.

The graph for the quilt *The Time Travellers*. Air Castle Star blocks are the "travellers" protected by the 54-40 or Fight blocks. Shoo-Fly blocks complete the design.

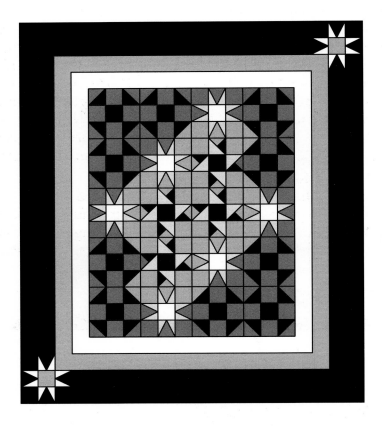

Shoo-Fly

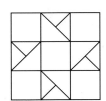

Air Castle Star

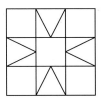

54-40 or Fight

blocks, pieced in myriad dark reds and blues, are the deep space through which the stars are moving.

While the interpretation of a *Stroll in the Garden* and *The Time Travellers* is personal to me as the designer, even a viewer not familiar with the making of these quilts, can recognize my intent. Movement and mood are conveyed through the choice of patterns, their placement within the quilt, and the use of color.

In conclusion, many methods may inspire you to combine different blocks. Compatible blocks may have a common shape or they may be cousins chosen from the same family of patterns. The blocks may be different, like **X** versus **O** blocks. You may choose certain blocks for your own sentimental reasons or use multiple blocks to spice up scrap quilts or to mark the passage of time, as in a calendar quilt. Allowing yourself to use different blocks in the same quilt gives the designer more freedom to express feelings, convey a mood, or illustrate a concept such as movement.

These methods for combining blocks can aid you in your choices for Crosspatch quilts. Draw at least a nine-block study before you begin to cut cloth. Planning at this stage will save you indecision later. Remember, it's only paper; not a single scrap of precious fabric has been wasted.

When quiltmakers hear the term "medallion quilts," they naturally make a mental association with the masterpiece medallion quilts made in the 18th and 19th century. These quilts were sophisticated and formal pieces. The typical medallion featured a prominent center design, such as a Tree of Life motif, then some open areas embellished with fancy quilting, and finally one or more borders often composed of pieced patterns. However, taken in a broader sense, a medallion quilt could be defined as follows: A quilt constructed in any combination of patterns that, through color placement and dark and light delineation, directs the viewer's attention to the center of the quilt. Other elements within the quilt reinforce, and do not distract, from this focus.

With that broad concept of a medallion, we can adapt the medallion style to a Crosspatch quilt. Looking at a study of a Crosspatch quilt and separating out the three parts of the design will enable you to design a medallion one step at a time. This simplification of how to design a medallion can be carried on in other quilt patterns. At the very least, the idea of designing a medallion should never again intimidate you.

The most important block of a medallion quilt is its center block. If the center does not attract and hold the viewer's attention, it is not a successful medallion. For instance, in a

Crosspatch study of nine blocks, the center could be pieced in only two fabrics, a dramatic contrast of light and dark, or display a flickering accent of a bright color that appears no other place in the quilt. A center block also could attract attention by being pieced in uncommon colors or by featuring an unusual print (illustration 23).

The second part of the design to consider is the four corner blocks. To make the process simpler, only design one of the corners. When you are satisfied with your corner block, then the

other three are pieced exactly alike and moved into their appropriate places in the design. Designing medallion-style means that the corner blocks are often pieced to reflect a diagonal line across the block. In this way, the part of the corner that touches the center block reinforces that center, while the outside edges of the corner blocks relate more to the borders (illustration 24).

The third part of the Crosspatch study to look at when designing in a medallion style is the compass blocks.

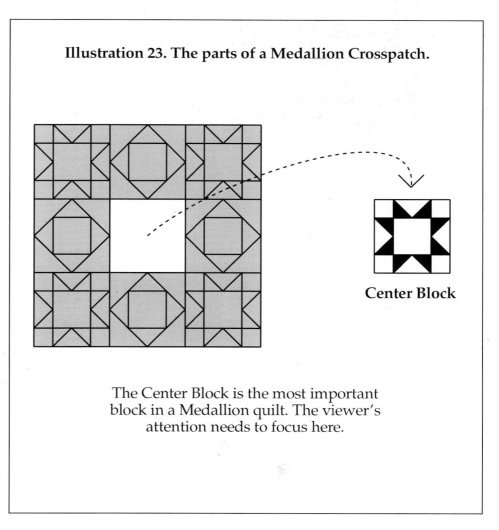

Illustration 23. The parts of a Medallion Crosspatch.

Center Block

The Center Block is the most important block in a Medallion quilt. The viewer's attention needs to focus here.

Illustration 24. The parts of a Medallion—*continued.* **Corner Blocks**

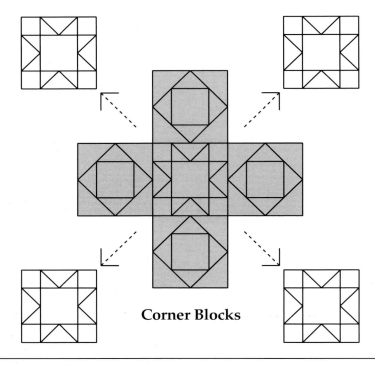

Corner Blocks

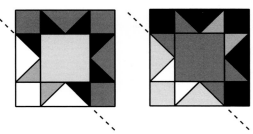

The corners need to stop the viewer's eye from leaving the quilt. Designed with a diagonal division across the block *(the result of fabric/color placement)*, they re-direct attention to the center.

Illustration 25. The parts of a Medallion—*continued.* **Compass Blocks**

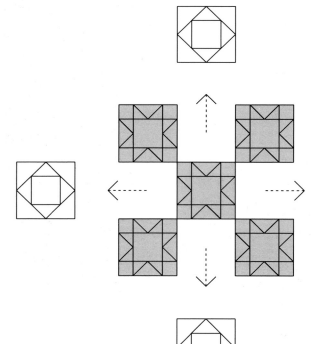

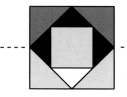

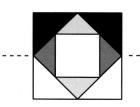

Compass blocks correspond to the North-South-East-West markers on a compass. Compass blocks often are designed to reflect a horizontal division across the block. They relate to the center but also begin the transition to the border.

Making Medallions in Crosspatch continued on page 41

THE QUILTS

1. Drunkard's Path

An example of the "Lend and Borrow" quilt designing style.
From Indiana, c. 1930, author's collection.

2. *Galaxy*

A Crosspatch quilt of Eccentric Star, Double Irish Chain, and
plain blocks. Designed by Pepper Cory, pieced by
Sherlee Mauch, quilted by an Amish Quilter.

3. *Dancing Chain*

Wall hanging of a Triple Irish Chain and Flying
Squares blocks. Made by Pepper Cory.

4. Twin Wall Hangings

Above left: *4A) Santa Fe* wall hanging. Made from Bear's Paw and complex Triple Irish Chain blocks.
Above right: *4B) Ohio Amish Bear's Paw* wall hanging inspired by Ohio Amish quilts. Bear's Paw with traditional Triple Irish Chain. Designed by Pepper Cory, pieced by Mary Remmington, Colleen Beach, and Marlene Eggert.

5. Portolani and Persian Fountains

Wall hangings combining Water Wheel and the octagon block from the Snowball pattern.
Above left: *5A) Portolani* designed by Pepper Cory, pieced by Gail Hill, quilted by Marlene Eggert.
Above right: *5B) Persian Fountains* designed by Pepper Cory, pieced and quilted by Colleen Beach.

6. *Valentine's Boogy and Stormy Weather*

Wall hangings that combine cousin blocks
Aunt Sukey's Choice and Wind Mill.

(Right)
6A) Valentine's Boogy designed and quilted by
Pepper Cory, pieced and bound by Marlene Eggert.

(Below)
6B) Stormy Weather designed by Pepper Cory, pieced by
Marlene Eggert, quilted by Norine Antuck, finishing by
Cindy Mielock.

7. *Fourth of July*

A Crosspatch wall hanging with Shoo-Fly and New
Kaleidoscope. Designed and pieced by Pepper Cory,
quilted by Louise Mueller.

8. Drought Series '88

Wall hangings combine King's X and Bachelor's Puzzle blocks.
Designed and pieced by Diana McGill. Collection of Diana McGill.

(Above)
8A)Ponds Drying in the Sun

(Right)
8B) Withered Wheat

(Below)
8C) The Rains Come Again.

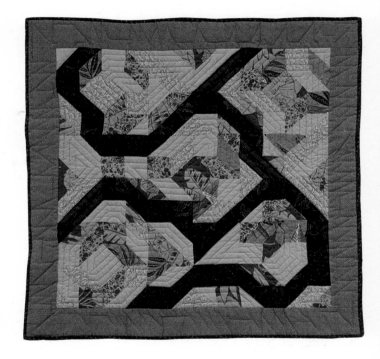

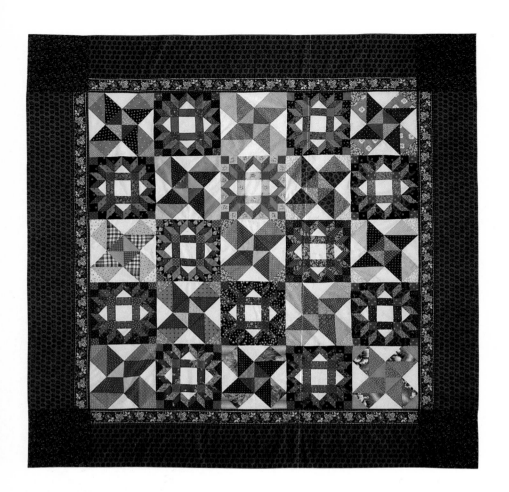

9. Shaylah's Quilt

A Crosspatch quilt top made for Shaylah Thornton. The blocks are Friendship Star and Next Door Neighbor. Designed by Pepper Cory, blocks and top made by members of the Capitol City Quilt Guild, Lansing, Michigan. Collection of Shaylah Thornton.

10. Marlene's Scrap Crosspatch

In planning her Nine Patch scrap quilt, Marlene Eggert used a Broken Dishes block to add accents of lighter color and to relieve the sameness of the Nine Patches. Collection of Marlene Eggert.

11. Calendar Quilt

A combination of Four Patch, representing Monday
through Saturday, and Puss-in-the-Corner, for Sunday.
This quilt was pieced, one block every day, in the fall of
1987. Designed and pieced by Pepper Cory, quilted by
Connie Hartwick, finishing by Jeanette Thayer.

12. Stroll in the Garden

A combination of blocks to convey a feeling of direction.
The Rolling Stone blocks stretch from upper right to lower
left, and six Crosspatch blocks contrast their "curves" to
the "path". The other blocks are Variable Star. Designed
by Pepper Cory, pieced by Gail Hill.

13. The Time Travellers

Three kinds of cousin blocks—Shoo-Fly, 54-40 or Fight, and Air Castle Star—combine in this piece. The idea of the quilt is to represent the movement of stars (the travellers) through space. The lighter red cloud around the travellers reinforces their relation to each other. Designed by Pepper Cory, pieced by Louis Mueller.

14A. Star Crossed

(Above left)
A medallion Crosspatch wall hanging with Sister's Choice and Shoo-Fly variation blocks. Design by Pepper Cory, quilt made by Beth Donaldson. Collection of Beth Donaldson.

14B. The Astronomer's Window

(Above right)
Crosspatch in the Out of Bounds style using Sister's Choice and Shoo-Fly variation blocks. Designed and pieced by Pepper Cory, quilted by Norine Antuck.

15. On The Road to Timbuktu

(Right)
A Medallion Crosspatch made from Prosperity and Night and Noon blocks. Design by Pepper Cory, border design and piecing by Bonnie Bus. Collection of Bonnie Bus.

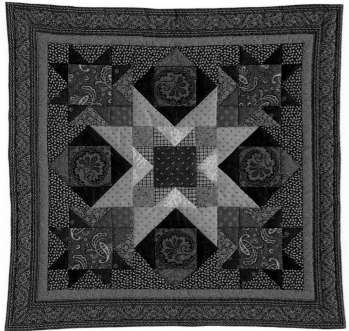

16. Wanda's Medallion

Medallion Crosspatch of Ohio Star and Economy Patch blocks. Design by Pepper Cory, pieced and quilted by Wanda Hansen. Collection of Wanda Hansen.

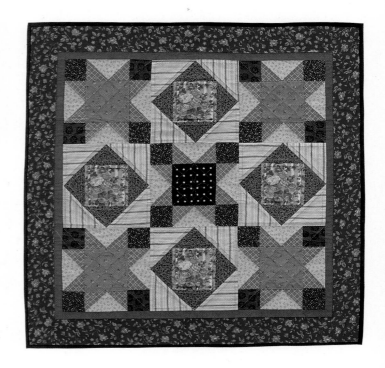

17A. X's and O's I

(Right center) Economy Patch and Ohio Star. Designed and pieced by Pepper Cory, quilting by Nancy Myers.

17B. Star Wars

(Below left) Medallion Crosspatch of Ohio Star and Economy Patch blocks. Designed by Pepper Cory, quilted and pieced by Gail Hill.

17C. Out of Bounds I

(Below right) Economy Patch and Ohio Star. Designed and pieced by Pepper Cory, quilted by Carol Seamon.

18. Nile Tile

Medallion Crosspatch that began as a study of Prickly Pear and
Four in the Corner blocks. Re-set as a medallion, Crow's Nest
blocks and pieced half-squares enlarged the quilt. Designed by
Pepper Cory, pieced by Norine Antuck, quilted by an Amish
quilter, finished by Jeanette Thayer.

19. Swing-in-the-Middle Medallions

(Above)

A) *Primo*—center block Ohio Star, corners—Crooked Road, compass blocks—Puss-in-the-Corner. Designed by Pepper Cory, pieced by Ann Snyder, quilted by Nancy Myers.

(Above right)

B) *Sub Rosa*—center block Economy Patch, corners—Northern Star, compass blocks—Double Four Patch. Designed by Pepper Cory, pieced and quilted by Judy Schimmel.

(Right center)

C) *Green Flightpath*—center block Economy Patch, corners—Dutchman's Puzzle, compass blocks—Bow Tie. Designed by Pepper Cory, pieced and quilted by Judy Schimmel.

20. UFO's Over Pensacola

Crosspatch wall hanging in the "Out of Bounds" style combines Nine Patch with Jacob's Ladder. Designed and pieced by Pepper Cory, quilted by Marlene Eggert.

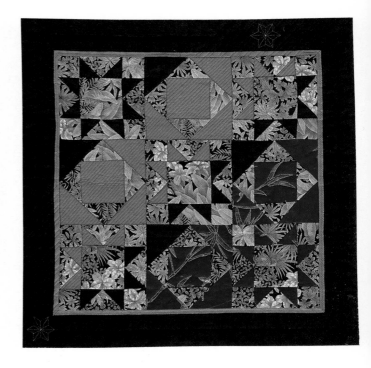

21. *Fractured Jungle and Terry's Stars*

Combinations of Ohio Star and Economy Patch. Design by Pepper Cory.

(Above left)
A) Fractured Jungle by Jill Stolpestad.

(Above right)
B) Terry's Stars by Terry McKenney-Person.

22. *Dolly Quilt*

(Right)
A combination of Checkerboard plus Log Cabin blocks. Northern Indiana, c. 1900. From the collection of Pepper Cory and Rebecca Haarer.

23. *Aloe Pots in the Window*

(Below)
The pattern resulted from combining a LeMoyne Star with a Card Trick block. Designed and pieced by Pepper Cory, quilted by Terry McKenney-Person.

24. *Wright Brothers Birds*

A combination of Birds in the Air and Log Cabin.
Designed and pieced by Pepper Cory, quilted by
Jeanette Hartwick, finished by Jeanette Thayer.

25. *Chef's Night Out*

Combination of Birds in the Air and Log Cabin. Design
by Pepper Cory, additional designing, piecing, and
quilting by Bonnie Bus. Collection of Bonnie Bus.

26. Lots o' Blocks

A Crosspatch of a Sixteen Patch with Cube Work blocks.
Designed and pieced by Pepper Cory, quilted by Gail Hill.

Making Medallions continued from page 24.

"Compass blocks" are the blocks in the design that would correspond to the North-South-East-West points on a compass. Compass blocks, like the corners, should magnify the middle of the quilt, and yet, also start a transition to the borders. Often compass blocks seem to have a horizontal line across them as they accomplish their dual purpose in the quilt (illustration 25).

*T*he quilt *Star Crossed* by Beth Donaldson combines Sister's Choice with a Shoo-Fly variation block. The center block floats in a dreamy gray and peach square. All the other blocks—the corners and the compass blocks—lay echoing frames around the center while toward the borders, the colors grow darker and darker. This is a very successful medallion in that it grabs your attention while it also features an illusion of light and dark (illustration 26, photo 14A).

A nine-block study of the patterns Prosperity and Night and Noon made for an interesting quilt called *On the Road to Timbuktu*. These blocks combined well since they both have right triangles in their corners. The quilt's maker, Bonnie Bus, used light-colored continuations from the Night and Noon blocks to construct her jagged "road" around the central design and added pieced borders (illustration 27, photo 15).

*S*ome medallions in the combination of Ohio Star and Economy Patch are *Star Wars* and *Wanda's Medallion*. Wanda Hansen's quilt, machine pieced and quilted in two days (!) was a

Illustration 26.

A Crosspatch study that alternates Sister's Choice blocks with a Shoo-Fly variation. The Medallion, *Star Crossed*, was designed from this study, as well as the Out of Bounds quilt, *The Astronomer's Window* (photos 14A and B).

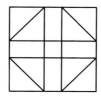
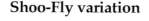
Shoo-Fly variation

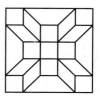
Sister's Choice

prize winner at the fair for her (photo 16 and photo 17). Refer to illustration 1 for graphs of these quilts.

*D*iana McGill's *Drought Series '88* quilts were designed with the X and O blocks of King's X and Bachelor's Puzzle. The first quilt, *Ponds Drying in the Sun*, is in the medallion style. The center block, outlined in dark brown, seems to be the last life-giving pool of water. The other drying ponds are light blue and seem to blend into the brown border (photo 8A).

*N*ile Tile was a medallion that grew from a nine-block study of Prickly Pear and Four in the Corner blocks. I hung the study from one corner in a diamond fashion on my bulletin board. It reminded me of the set of an Amish Center Diamond quilt. I drafted complimentary blocks, a simpler version of Prickly Pear called Crow's Nest, and pieced half-squares. My friend, Norine

Antuck, who had made the study in the first place, was willing to piece its new, improved version. In this quilt, a Crosspatch study served as the medallion's center and it inspired the other blocks which extended the size of the quilt (illustration 28, photo 18).

*T*hree small quilts in a style I call Swing-in-the-Middle were the result of experimenting in Crosspatch medallions. Like other medallions, their designs focused on a center block but then the designs branch out in paths from the middle (illustration 29, photo 19). The feeling in these quilts reminded me of a square dance maneuver called "Swing in the Middle" where couples come together for a turn in the middle of the dance floor but then swing away, each with a new partner. In a Swing-in-the-Middle medallion, the center

Illustration 27.

The study for *On the Road to Timbuktu* (photo 15) combines Prosperity with Night and Noon blocks.

Prosperity   **Night and Noon**

Illustration 28. The graph for the quilt *Nile Tile*.

A nine block study of Prickly Pear and Four in the Corner, used as a center diamond, was expanded with Crow's Nest blocks and a pieced half-block.

Pieced half-block   **Prickly Pear**

Crow's Nest   **Four in the Corner**

42

block should be a symmetrical block, such as Economy Patch or Ohio Star. The corner blocks have a definite direction, while the compass blocks are simple patterns. Swing-in-the-Middle designs are an intriguing sub-group of medallions. These quilts are only small samples of the possibilities when Crosspatch blocks are handled in a medallion style.

When you apply Crosspatch to a medallion, the basic premise of a central focus to the quilt should be evident. All the other blocks need to magnify and con-tain the center. Medallions are an enormously challenging area of Crosspatch design. They force us to view the quilt as a whole, make us step back to admire the interplay of line and color, while at the same time, they beckon us closer to examine the design at their heart.

Illustration 29. Studies for Medallion variations called *Swing-in-the-Middle* quilts (photo 19).

A) Primo

Center: Ohio Star

Corners: Crooked Road

Compass blocks: Puss in the Corner

B) Sub Rosa

Center: Economy Patch

Corners: Northern Star

Compass blocks: Four Patch

C) Green Flightpath

Center: Economy Patch

Corners: Dutchman's Puzzle

Compass blocks: Bow Tie

OUT OF BOUNDS

Many traditional quiltmakers are in awe of contemporary quilts. We may admire the quilts, but think, "Oh, I could never do something like that"! Many of us use only traditional patterns and tried-and-true block arrangements. We personalize our quilts by using colors and fabrics we like.

Perhaps a traditional quilter, however, might venture into a contemporary approach to quiltmaking if she didn't have to give up the fabrics she loved and wasn't obliged to learn new and difficult techniques. But what if all that was required to make a contemporary quilt was a different point of view? Wouldn't you be more likely to try one, if all you had to do was look at your quiltmaking process from a different perspective?

A designing approach that I call "Out of Bounds" could be a traditional quilter's bridge to contemporary quilts. For instance, I had drawn a nine-block study of Nine Patch and Jacob's Ladder. The combination of cousin blocks seemed almost too elementary to be interesting. How was I going to add some "spice" to this design? A wild fabric—one of those "someday I'll use it" treasures—was the answer. The fabric was a Hawaiian floral of orchids and greenery on a white background. I cut out squares and right triangles from the Hawaiian fabric and using a flannel board as my design surface, I scattered the shapes throughout the Nine Patch and Jacob's Ladder blocks. I cut more shapes in the floral print, and the distinction between Nine Patches and Jacob Ladders seem to fragment before my eyes. With four coordinating solids—magenta, two shades of green, and lavender—I filled in the remaining holes of the design. The diagonal rows of colors seemed to float above a tropical scene. Thus *UFO's Over Pensacola* was born (illustration 30, photo 20).

Another Out of Bounds is the fraternal twin to *Star Crossed*, the medallion quilt in photo 14A. This piece is entitled *The Astronomer's Window* (photo 14B).

Other quilts in the Out of Bounds style are variations of the Ohio Star and Economy Patch combination (photo 17C, photo 21 A and B).

These are suggestions for designing in the Out of Bounds style.

- ❏ Draw a study of simple blocks and follow it as you cut and lay down fabrics.
- ❏ Start with a wild or large-scale print as your first fabric.
- ❏ Do not allow the seams of the blocks to limit your color placement.
- ❏ Perceive your study as an overall design that contains many different shapes. Don't think of your quilt as different quilt blocks set side by side.
- ❏ Do not feel you have to use the same fabric in the same place in every block.
- ❏ Keep manipulating the pieces until you are satisfied with the whole look of the quilt.
- ❏ Make your final decisions from a distance. Back up and view the piece from 7 to 10 feet away rather than nose-to-the-fabric.

Designing from the "big picture", you can move color and pattern beyond the boundaries of the blocks.

Out of Bounds is a stylistic attitude rather than a readily identifiable characteristic. It consists of a good quilt plan, a weird and wonderful fabric, and an open mind. Even if you are a traditional quiltmaker you can design a modern quilt. And you will feel justifiably proud as you finally find a use for that "funny" fabric that's been on the shelf for years.

Illustration 30.
A study of simple blocks that became *UFO's over Pensacola*
in the Out of Bounds style (photo 20).

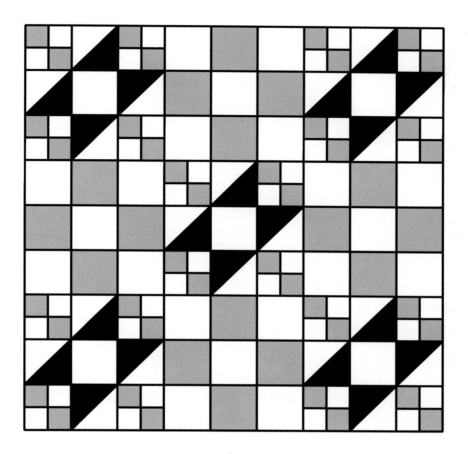

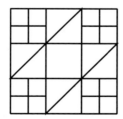

Jacob's Ladder

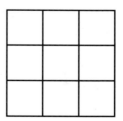

Nine Patch

Illustration 31.
The graph of the antique *Dolly Quilt* (photo 22).

The Dolly Quilt has a Checkerboard block as its center and uses Log Cabin and Courthouse Steps blocks cut in half to combine in this unique design.

A suggestion for multiplying the Dolly Quilt graph as a larger quilt.

Checkerboard

Log Cabin

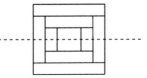

Courthouse Steps

I am very glad that there actually is a word that describes what I call "happy accidents", those unsought discoveries that just happen as you are busily pursuing some other interest.

*A*t an antique show, my friend, Rebecca, and I saw a dolly quilt at the same time. We both admired it, she for its diminutive charm, I for its use of two patterns. Made around 1900, the quilter had combined a Checkerboard block with two kinds of Log Cabin blocks. Maybe a little girl begged her Momma for a quilt for her doll, so Momma dipped into her quilt blocks and snip! snip!—a dolly quilt done. In the case of this little Crosspatch sample, one of the patterns, the Checkerboard, is complete. Two Log Cabin blocks, cut on the diagonal, expand the Checkerboard from a diamond to a square. A third block, a Courthouse Steps variation, cut in half, makes a rectangle of the pieces (illustration 31, photo 22). After I drafted the dolly quilt design and played with rearranging it, my respect for the quiltmaker rose. It is a good design!

*O*nce I realized that the quilt block patterns themselves were not sacred, I began to experiment with the idea of constructing new patterns from parts of other patterns.

I went back to the tracing paper drawings of blocks I had made in my Crosspatch research. Opening the folder of drawings, I noticed that, due to the translucency of the tracing

Illustration 32.

Research in Crosspatch designs yielded an unexpected result when drawings of two traditional blocks on tracing paper overlapped and formed a new block.

LeMoyne Star

Cardtrick

The new block

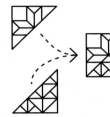

The new block has complex piecing.

Separating the drawings to a diagonal half of each pattern.

The new block named Aloe Pot, with the piecing in the lower half of the block simplified for easier construction.

The graph for the *Aloe Pots* wall hanging (photo 23).

Illustration 33.

Two traditional quilt blocks, Birds in the Air and Log Cabin, combine as a new pattern.

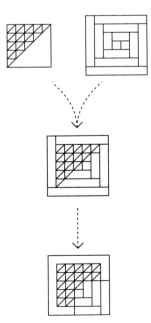

The combination block.
The block, simplified for easier piecing, is named Wright Brothers Birds.

Illustration 34.

The graph for the quilts *Wright Brothers Birds* and *Chef's Night Out* (photos 24 and 25).

Illustration 35.
Study for *Lots o' Blocks*, a Crosspatch that alternates a two-dimensional pattern,
Sixteen Patch, with its three-dimensional version, Cube Work.

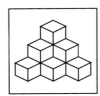

Cube Work. The "cubes" are pieced
from 60° diamonds, then appliquéd
on the background block.

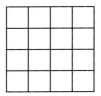

Sixteen Patch

the translucency of the tracing paper, the block designs from underneath the top copy were showing through. The lines from underneath intersected with lines on the top block emerging into new shapes. Thus new patterns were born from two traditional blocks.

Several of these by-products of Crosspatch research were irresistible patterns. One that made it into cloth was a hybrid I called *Aloe Pot*. The leaves of the aloe plant are one-half of a LeMoyne Star while the "pot" is half of a Card Trick block. When the two different halves came together, they merge as a new addition to the family of basket patterns (illustration 32, photo 23). In the wall hanging, blocks are

in a row similar to the way you see aloes lined up on many American windowsills.

Another new pattern was a combination of Birds-in-the-Air and Log Cabin. I named the new pattern *Wright Brothers Birds* (illustration 33). The name refers to all the Wright brothers who are heroes of mine—Wilbur, Orville, and Frank Lloyd. I doubt Frank Lloyd visualized quilts in his houses; however, the designs and color interplay of patchwork are part of every American artist's cultural background. Because she liked the design, my friend, Bonnie Bus, took the graph of Wright Brothers Birds and made her own version. Using a 1950s print showing wine bottles, skillets, cooks (complete with peaked hats) and even dancing pigs, she named

her quilt *Chef's Night Out* (illustration 34, photos 24 and 25).

My perception of how to design quilts has been permanently broadened. Even the idea of combining two and three-dimensional versions of the same block is not off-limits. The quilt called *Lots o' Blocks* is the result of that speculation (illustration 35, photo 26). It combines a flat-looking block of sixteen squares with an adjoining block showing the squares as cubes. Crosspatch has rejuvenated my whole attitude toward quiltmaking and it keeps me interested in working. My wish for you is that your quilt designing will also be inspired as a result of Crosspatch experiments.

A Personal Color Confidence Worksheet

Whether you work in a studio, a sewing room, or out of a basket of scraps in your lap, you go through a series of choices while working on a quilt. Chief among these is the selection of fabrics.

I personally use the "scenario" method for choosing colors, and this has worked well for many quilters. It is not a technical method based on color-wheel formulas, but rather bases color selection on how a color, or combinations of colors, makes one feel. Any quilter can discover and define her natural color preferences and use this knowledge to help her focus her color choices. The purpose of this exercise is to analyze your existing color preferences and dislikes. It is not designed to change your mind about color—just assist you in looking at the role of color in your life.

When you have finished your **Personal Color Confidence Worksheet** (*see next page*), don't forget to date it. Your color preferences may change over time, and it will be interesting to you to have a record of your growth.

The Worksheet helps you realize who you are in relation to colors, and the following tips can assist you in using that knowledge.

When you consciously are playing with color in your quilts, choose a simple piecing pattern, even an old, familiar block you have made before. Make quilts to suit *your* personal color preferences. You will be happier as you quilt and with the resulting piece. If making a quilt for someone else, ask the quilt's recipient what their favorite colors are. As you plan that quilt, combine their preferences with at least one color you really love. That beloved color will get you through a lot of tedious work.

As you experiment, make variations of the same pattern but use different colors. Look at your variations and continue multiplying the one you like best into a quilt. Leave the rest of the sample blocks for later, for someone else to do, or for your children to find. Before you dash off to the fabric store to buy new fabrics, look at the fabrics you already have. Turn the stacks upside down. Shuffle the fabrics so that the latest fabrics change position with old fabrics. Trade a few of your "oldies but goodies" with a friend. Take ten or twenty of the dark fabrics and fold them inside out so that you are looking at their grayed version. Navy blues will blur into soft gray, red to pink, mustard gold to tan, etc. Lastly, try the "Piece of This, Piece of That" formula. Does your quilt design call for red? In the red places, try a little piece of a wide variety of red prints—even a different red for every red piece indicated in the plan of your quilt. This adds richness and complexity to your quilt without your having to constantly make choices—just reach into your reds and cut!

Personal Color Confidence Worksheet

I. Your colors

Color(s) I Love

_____
_____
_____
_____

Color(s) I Hate

_____
_____
_____
_____

Color(s) I Love could be defined as colors that, if they were a flavor, would be delicious. *Color(s) I Hate* produce a strong antipathy—they make you say "yuck!".

Color(s) I Wear

_____
_____
_____
_____

Color(s) I Live With

_____
_____
_____
_____

Color(s) I Wear can be influenced by the job you do, the community in which you live, and your age. *Color(s) I Live With* are often compromises—the old carpet that's still too good to throw out, the color of your husband's favorite easy chair and so on.

Have you taken any "Color Me Beautiful" classes or read that book?

❏ Yes   ❏ No

If you have, did the experience change your clothing color preferences?

❏ Yes   ❏ No

Do you agree with the "Color Me Beautiful" analysis of your taste?

❏ Yes   ❏ No

II. Changes and Shifts

Sometimes when we consider our color options, like when we're standing staring at our stacks of fabrics searching for inspiration in our next quilt, we discover our color preferences have changed. Sometimes slightly, other times radically. What within us has precipitated these changes? What influences outside of ourselves come to bear on our color choices?

Choices within us—List some personal changes you've gone through in the past five years. These might include a move, a job change, a divorce or death, a marriage, a birth, a child leaving home for college, recovery from an illness, etc.

_____
_____
_____
_____

Outside influences—List some influences (different than the ones listed above) that may have affected your color preferences. Some influences might be decorating or quilt magazines, a person in your life with strong opinions, etc.

_____
_____
_____
_____

Do you remember a particular incident or experience that had a profound influence on your color preference? Briefly describe it.

_____
_____
_____
_____
_____

III. Color Choice by Intuition/Inspiration

The idea here is to group colors, acting on knowledge we already have. Look at the following scenarios that you can use as inspirations in planning your quilt color schemes. Write next to the scenario the names of colors you visualize as you think of the little scene. Remember that artistic expression is your intuitive response to interior feelings-so don't think with your head but feel with your heart!

Sunset at the Beach _____

Winter Landscape _____

Prom Night _____

A Tropical Island _____

My Favorite Holiday _____

Walk in the Garden _____

IV. Add a scenario title of your own and list the colors it suggests

_____
_____
_____

V. Suggestions for remembering color combinations:

A follow-up exercise to this worksheet is some homework. Get some 3" x 5" blank file cards, a glue stick, a pair of scissors, and a pile of fabrics and scraps. Don't do any pre-sorting of the fabrics—dump it all out on the table—and go for it. Think of a scenario, title your card on the back, and cut small snippets of cloth that represent your interpretation of the scenario. Better to cut a lot than just a few. Arrange your snippets and glue them on the card. Viola! A color palette, a "recipe" for a new quilt, custom picked by and for *you*.

VI. Can you draw any conclusions about your color preferences?

_____
_____

Are you satisfied with why and how you choose colors?

_____

Do you foresee any color changes coming for you?

_____
_____

How to Draft (almost) Any Pattern the Size You Want

The method described here is useful for drafting geometric patchwork patterns. When you see patterns you would like to combine in Crosspatch, the blocks may not always be the same size.

One way to avoid drafting for the blocks in Crosspatch quilts is to do what I did—take the easy way out. If for example, the blocks I wanted to combine all came from the nine-patch family, I drew a square that was 6", 9" or 12" on each side. I al-ways kept the block size a multi-ple of three. But what if, at some future time, you need to draft a nine-patch pattern in a 10" size? The graph paper hasn't been in-vented that will solve that prob-lem and a calculator, endlessly punching out 3.3333 is no help (illustration 36).

The problem of drawing a nine-patch pattern in a 10" square is simplified when you realize a 10" square is composed of four 10" lines. These are the sides of the square. If all the 10" lines can be divided into three equal divisions and marked with dots, then new lines can be drawn between the dots. The new lines will result in a nine-patch grid in a 10" square. To make this drawing, you will need a pencil, an eraser, a large sheet of plain white paper (large means bigger than 10", plain means *not* graph paper), a straight-edge longer than a one foot ruler (clear plastic quilt rulers are good, as well as the ever-popular wooden yardstick from the local hardware store), and a large plastic drafting tri-angle or a carpenter's square (il-lustration 37). Follow the directions in illustration 38.

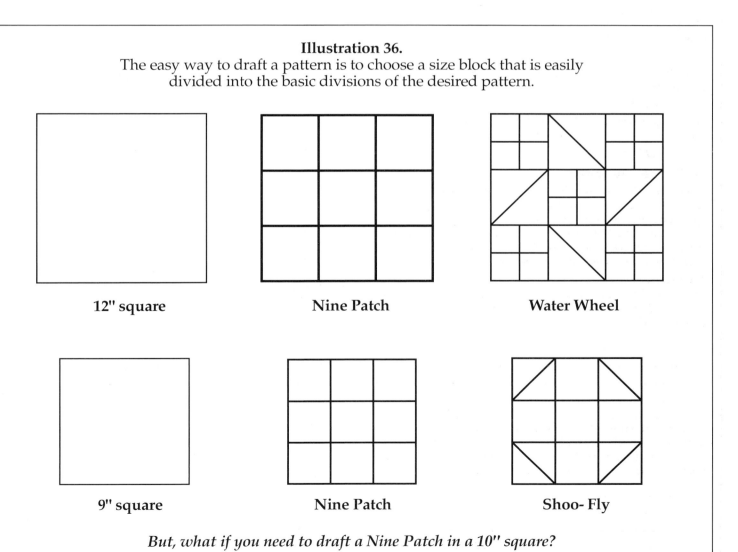

Illustration 36.
The easy way to draft a pattern is to choose a size block that is easily divided into the basic divisions of the desired pattern.

12" square

Nine Patch

Water Wheel

9" square

Nine Patch

Shoo- Fly

But, what if you need to draft a Nine Patch in a 10" square?

Illustration 37.
A 10" square is made up of four 10" lines.

If you can divide the 10" lines in three equal divisions, mark the divisions on the lines, then draw connecting lines, you can get a Nine Patch in a 10" square. You will need a large sheet of plain white paper, a pencil with an eraser, a quilting ruler or yardstick, and a large drafting triangle or a carpenter's square.

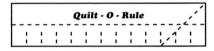

Lemon Bros. Hardware ⌇ Barnwell, S. Carolina

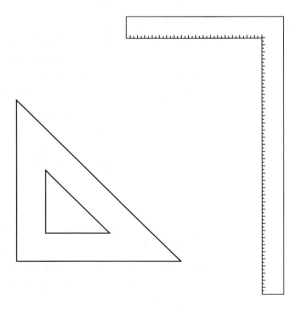

Save your nine-patch in a 10" square drawing. In the future when you need another nine-patch type of pattern in a 10" size, all you will have to do is take out your original, place tracing paper over it, draw the basic grid, and then complete the desired block.

In the future, if you need to draw a pattern for a block in a size you do not have, remember these guidelines:

- Look at a picture of the block you would like to draw. Ask yourself, "Is this block basically a nine-patch, five-patch, four-patch etc.?" You will need to know this so that you can later divide lines by three, five, or four.

- Draw a square the same size as the block you want to use.

- Follow the steps in illustration 38. The logic is the same whether you are drawing a Sister's Choice (a five-patch) in a 12" square or a Water Wheel (nine-patch) in a 10" square.

This method of reproducing patterns is called proportional spacing, and it will prove useful to you as you consider different combinations of blocks in Crosspatch quilts. It is difficult to always find the patterns you want in the same size. But if you are able to draw the blocks yourself with a minimum of effort, your choices for Crosspatch can

Illustration 38.
How to Get a Nine-Patch in a 10" Block

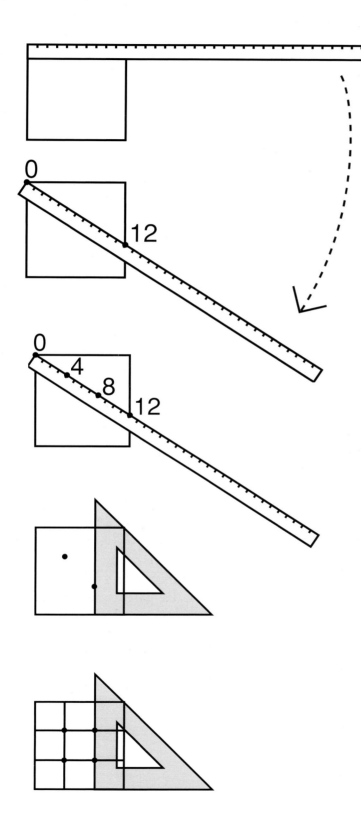

1. Draw an accurate 10" square on the plain paper. Make sure the corners are perpendicular lines, the square straight on the paper, and all four sides of the square are 10" long.

2. Because you are drafting a Nine-patch *(three divisions across by three divisions down)* think of a number that is a multiple of three but larger than 10, such as 12.

3. Place the 0 of the straightedge at the upper left corner of the 10" square, and then swing the straightedge down to the right until the 12" marker intersects exactly the right side of the square.

4. Since 12 divided by 3 is 4, as you look along the straightedge from 0 to 12", mark a dot every four inches. You will make a dot at 4" and another at 8".

5. Using either the large triangle or carpenter's square, align the bottom of the triangle or square with the bottom line of the 10" square. Move the tool so that its perpendicular side exactly intersects the first dot at 4". Using the tool as a straightedge, draw a line up to the top of the square from the dot and down to the bottom of the square. Move the tool to the 8" dot and repeat. Half the lines for a nine-patch are now complete.

6. Turn the drawing so the new lines are horizontal in the square. Begin with Step 3 and repeat the process to make the remaining lines. When you have finished, you will have nine equal divisions in your 10" square.

include almost any patchwork pattern that exists.

Making Templates

You will need to make templates to cut out your Crosspatch blocks. There are some patterns given in this book, and while you might want to photocopy the patterns, be aware that photocopying generally distorts the image. A square may turn out to be one-eighth of an inch larger than its original. The copy can even subtly change a square to a rectangle. In most cases, drafting your own patterns or tracing directly from the book is preferable.

To make templates, lay a piece of template plastic over the patterns in the book. I prefer a 15 millimeter (.015) translucent mylar. It is thin enough to see through and cut with scissors, but thick enough to make sturdy templates. These templates may even be used with a quilt ruler and rotary cutter. In that case, slip the template under the ruler, carefully aligning the edge of the template with the edge of the ruler and run the cutter alongside the edge as you usually do. Before cutting out templates, draw the lines of the pattern with a permanent marker. Use a marker that dries quickly and will not smear on plastic (see Supplies). If you handpiece and prefer your templates exact size, draw only the inside (sewing) line, and cut out. Cut the template out using

the outside lines (one quarter inch seam allowance) as your guide if you machine piece. Mark a dot on your machine template where any sewing lines intersect to ensure precision piecing. With a ⅛" or 1/16" hole punch, punch a little hole in the plastic at that spot. Dot the fabrics through the holes with a washable marker or pencil after you have drawn around your templates on the fabric. As you machine sew, use the dot-to-dot guide and a ¼ inch seam indicator, such as a ¼ inch wide piece of masking tape on the plate of your sewing machine, to ensure accurate sewing.

Cutting

Mark around the templates and cut the fabrics out according to your preference. The ↔ lines on the templates indicate grain lines. However, if you do not choose to follow the grain lines because you want to cut your fabric to capture a particular part of the print, that's okay too. You can use "off-grain" pieces as long as you are aware that your piece may have several bias edges, and you handle it carefully to avoid stretching as you sew. If the fabric from which you are cutting an off-grain piece is flimsy, lightly spray the fabric with sizing, press, then cut the piece. The wobbly fabric will be stabilized enough to handle.

Piecing

Use a running stitch to sew the pieces when you are hand-piecing. Generally match the piecing thread to the darker fabric. Use straight pins to pin pieces at the intersections and

sew on marked lines. While you should knot your thread to secure at the beginning of stitching, you may backstitch 2 to 3 stitches to end.

When machine piecing, use the ¼ inch guide to sew by. Use a poly/cotton or all cotton sewing weight (#50) thread in both the bobbin and on top. Backstitch a stitch or two at the beginning and end of a seam to secure.

Order of Piecing

Almost always, piece a block in order of its smallest to its largest units. Get the smallest pieces out of the way first, then assemble the block in rows, and then sew the rows. Do not immediately sew block to block, but complete all the blocks, then take some time to play with the order of the blocks before assembling the whole quilt in its final form. This will be your last chance to change the look of your piece. If you want to keep track of the blocks in their original positions, put a small piece of masking tape on the back of each block and mark it "Number One" and so on. Remove the tape indicators when you have stitched the blocks together in their final design.

The technicalities of sewing, basting, and quilting are not thoroughly explained here because most people who are interested in Crosspatch will already be quilters. But if, as you are making Crosspatch, any technical difficulties should arise, refer to one of the excellent texts available on basic quiltmaking (*see Bibliography*).

*A*ll of us, at one time or another, have a desire to make a quilt uniquely our own. A quilt different than the quilts we commonly make, a masterpiece that will make the viewer stop and look, and look again. A quilt that will make another quilter say, "That looks like so-and-so's work", as surely as if our name was signed across the bottom of the quilt. Is it wishful thinking that you could make a quilt like that? I think not. In the designing process, good design and the ability to focus your creativity is 90 percent learnable. The other 10 percent—the desire to make better, more beautiful quilts—has to come from within. Since you have read this far, give yourself a star; you already have the desire to be a better quiltmaker.

Crosspatch was not meant to be a "How-To" book. Rather, **Crosspatch** is a "Why Not?" book offering inspiration, ideas, and the encouragement to experiment. My desire is that you will incorporate some of these ideas with your own skills and creativity to produce wonderful quilts that please you. **Crosspatch** was written because it was the book I searched for as I started to work with more than one pattern in my quilts. **Crosspatch** is my gift to the average quiltmaker, like me, who is looking for that spark to make their quilts special. I hope it will start you dreaming, designing, and doing.

CHART OF QUILT INFORMATION

Title of Quilt	Blocks Used in the Quilt	Chapter That Explains the Style	Illustration #	Photo
Aloe Pots	combination LeMoyne Star, Card Trick*	Serendipity	32	23
The Astronomer's Window	Sister's Choice*, Shoo-Fly variation*	Out of Bounds	26	14B
Calendar Quilt	Double Four Patch, Puss in the Corner	Choosing Blocks—Scrap Quilts	20	11
Chef's Night Out	combination Birds in the Air, Log Cabin	Serendipity	34	25
Dancing Chain	Triple Irish Chain, Flying Squares	Crosspatch Ancestors	9	3
Dolly Quilt	Checkerboard, Log Cabin, Courthouse Steps	Serendipity	31	22
Drunkard's Path	Drunkard's Path	Crosspatch—History	2	1
Fourth of July	Shoo Fly, New Kaleidoscope*	Choosing Blocks—Cousins	16	7
Fractured Jungle	Economy Patch*, Ohio Star*	Out of Bounds	1	21A
Galaxy	Eccentric Star*, Double Irish Chain	Crosspatch Ancestors	7	2
Green Flightpath	Economy Patch*, Dutchman's Puzzle, Bow Tie	Medallions—Swing-in-the-Middle	29	19C
Lots o' Blocks	Sixteen Patch, Cubework	Serendipity	35	26
Marlene's Scrap Quilt	Broken Dishes, Nine Patch	Choosing Blocks—Scrap Quilts	19	10
Nile Tile	Prickly Pear, Crow's Nest, Four in the Corner	Medallions	28	18
Ohio Amish Bear's Paw	Bear's Paw, Triple Irish Chain	Crosspatch Ancestors	10	4B
Out of Bounds I	Economy Patch*, Ohio Star*	Out of Bounds	1	17C
Persian Fountains	Water Wheel, Snowball	Crosspatch Ancestors	12	5B
Ponds Drying in the Sun	King's X*, Bachelor's Puzzle*	Choosing Blocks—X's and O's, Medallions	17	8A

*templates are given for these blocks

Title of Quilt	Blocks Used in the Quilt	Chapter That Explains the Style	Illustration #	Photo
Portolani	Water Wheel, Snowball	Crosspatch Ancestors	12	5A
Primo	Ohio Star*, Crooked Road, Puss in the Corner	Medallions—Swing- in-the-Middle	29	19A
The Rains Come Again	King's X*, Bachelor's Puzzle*	Choosing Blocks—X's and O's	17	8C
On the Road to Timbuktu	Prosperity, Night and Noon*	Medallions	27	15
Santa Fe	Bear's Paw, Triple Irish Chain	Crosspatch Ancestors	10	4A
Shaylah's Quilt	Friendship Star, Next Door Neighbor*	Choosing Blocks— Sentimental Reasons	18	9
Star Crossed	Sister's Choice*, Shoo-Fly variation*	Medallions	26	14A
Star Wars	Economy Patch*, Ohio Star*	Medallions	1	17B
Stormy Weather	Aunt Sukey's Choice*, Wind Mill	Choosing Blocks—Cousins	15	6B
Stroll in the Garden	Rolling Stone*, Crosspatch*, Variable Star*	Choosing Blocks—Artistic Intent	21	12
Sub Rosa	Economy Patch*, Northern Star, Four Patch	Medallions—Swing-in-the-Middle	29	19B
Terry's Stars	Economy Patch*, Ohio Star*	Out of Bounds	1	21B
The Time Travellers	Shoo Fly, 54-40 or Fight, Air Castle Star	Choosing Blocks—Artistic Intent	22	13
UFO's Over Pensacola	Nine Patch, Jacob's Ladder	Out of Bounds	30	20
Valentine's Boogy	Aunt Sukey's Choice*, Wind Mill	Choosing Blocks—Cousins	15	6A
Wanda's Medallion	Economy Patch*, Ohio Star*	Medallions	1	16
Withered Wheat	King's X*, Bachelor's Puzzle*	Out of Bounds	17	8B
Wright Brothers Birds	combination Birds in the Air, Log Cabin	Serendipity	34	24
X's and O's I	Economy Patch*, Ohio Star*	Choosing Blocks—X's and O's	1	17A

THE PATTERNS

The patterns for fifteen of the blocks used in the Crosspatch samples are given here. The blocks are all 12" square, and have both the sewing lines and the ¼" seam allowance lines.

The blocks are grouped together according to their basic construction. The nine-patch blocks are together, the four-patches together and so on.

These particular blocks were chosen because many of the samples used them, or the patterns are not easy to find in a 12" size. Very simple blocks, such as Nine Patch and Snowball, are not given since they are easy to draw. If you need guidance in drafting patterns, refer to *How to Draft (almost) Any Pattern in the Size You Want* in *Help in Making Crosspatch Quilts. (page 49)*

The following are the blocks for which the patterns are given:

Aloe Pot

Economy Patch

Ohio Star

Aunt Sukey's Choice

King's X

Rolling Stone

Bachelor's Puzzle

New Kaleidoscope

Shoo-Fly variation

Crosspatch

Next Door Neighbor

Sister's Choice

Eccentric Star

Night and Noon

Variable Star

Crosspatch (29 pieces)

N1: *cut 1*
N3: *cut 4*
N4: *cut 8*
N5: *cut 4*
N13: *cut 4*
N14: *cut 4*
N14 reverse: *cut 4*

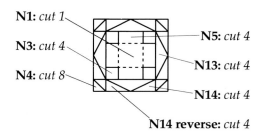

Aloe Pot (18 pieces)

N1: *cut 1*
N2: *cut 3*
N6: *cut 2*
N7: *cut 6*
N9: *cut 2*
N9 reverse: *cut 2*
N12: *cut 2*

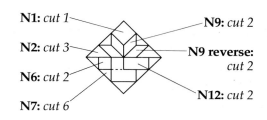

Aunt Sukey's Choice (37 pieces)

N1: *cut 1*
N3: *cut 16*
N4: *cut 8*
N7: *cut 4*
N10: *cut 4*
N10 reverse: *cut 4*

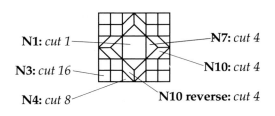

Rolling Stone (29 pieces)

N1: *cut 1*
N4: *cut 16*
N5: *cut 8*
N6: *cut 4*

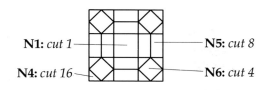

Variable Star (17 pieces)

N1: *cut 4*
N7: *cut 12*
N8: *cut 1*

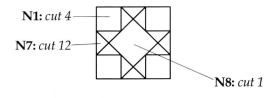

Bachelor's Puzzle (17 pieces)

N1: *cut 1*
N6: *cut 4*
N2: *cut 4*
N9: *cut 4*
N9 reverse: *cut 4*

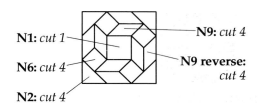

Night and Noon (29 pieces)

N4: *cut 8*
N7: *cut 12*
N8: *cut 1*
N11: *cut 4*
N11 reverse: *cut 4*

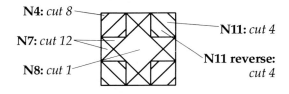

New Kaleidoscope (12 pieces)

N2: *cut 4*
N6: *cut 4*
N15: *cut 4*

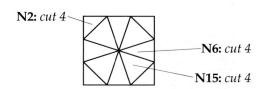

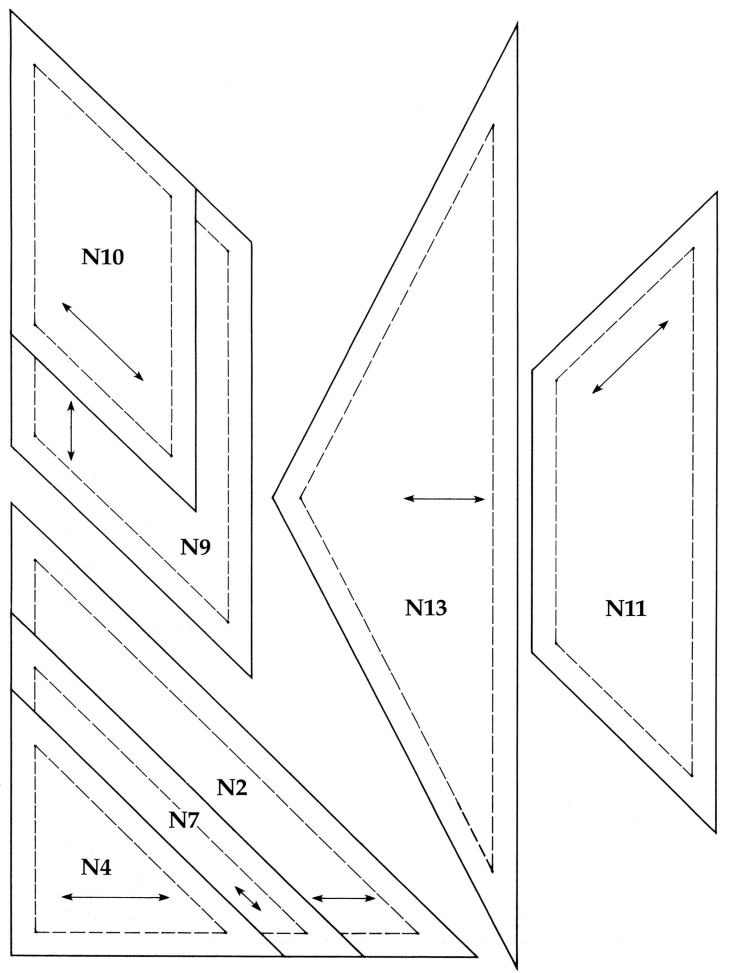

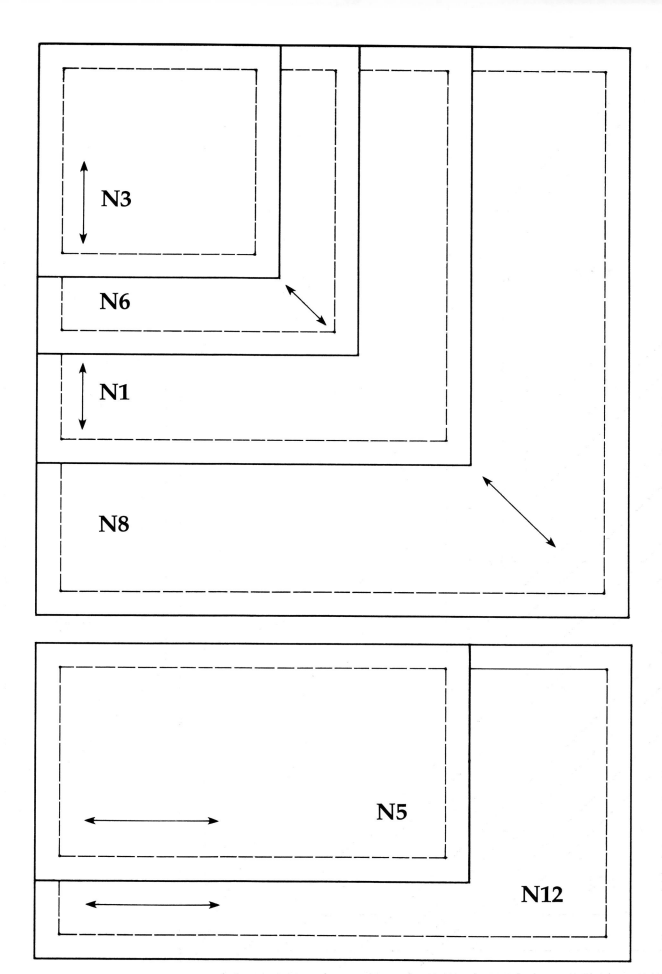

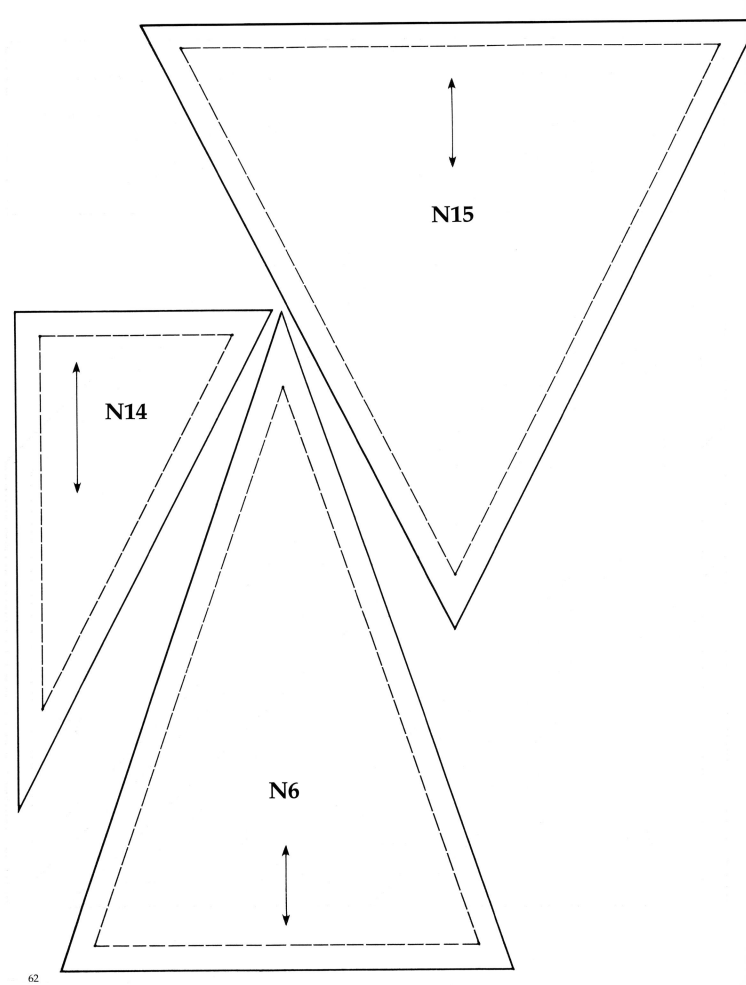

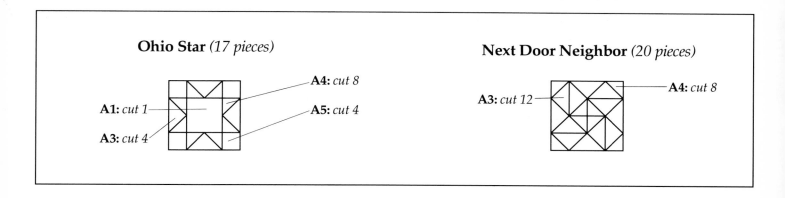

Ohio Star *(17 pieces)*

A1: *cut 1*
A3: *cut 4*
A4: *cut 8*
A5: *cut 4*

Next Door Neighbor *(20 pieces)*

A3: *cut 12*
A4: *cut 8*

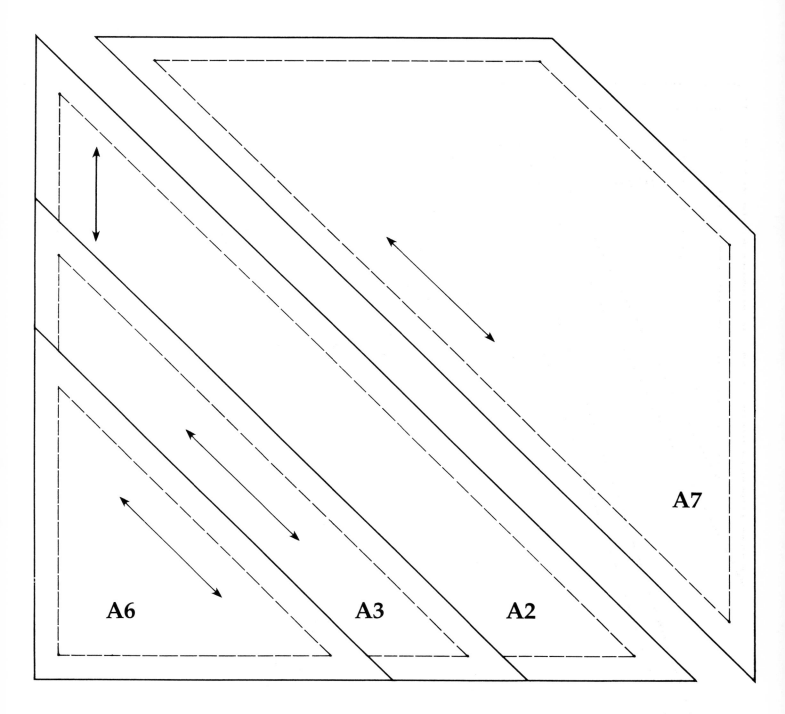

A7

A6

A3

A2

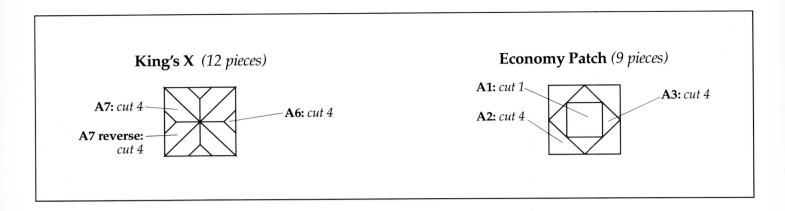

King's X *(12 pieces)*

A7: *cut 4*

A6: *cut 4*

A7 reverse: *cut 4*

Economy Patch *(9 pieces)*

A1: *cut 1*

A3: *cut 4*

A2: *cut 4*

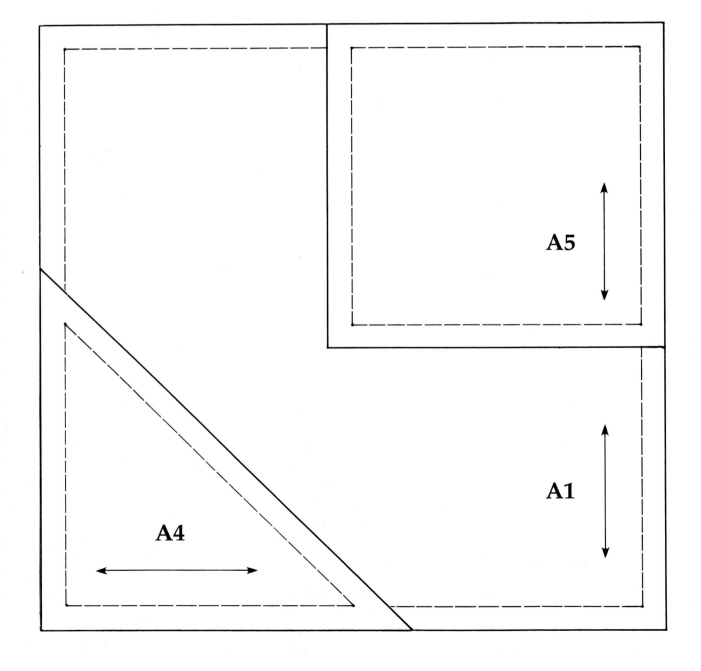

A5

A1

A4

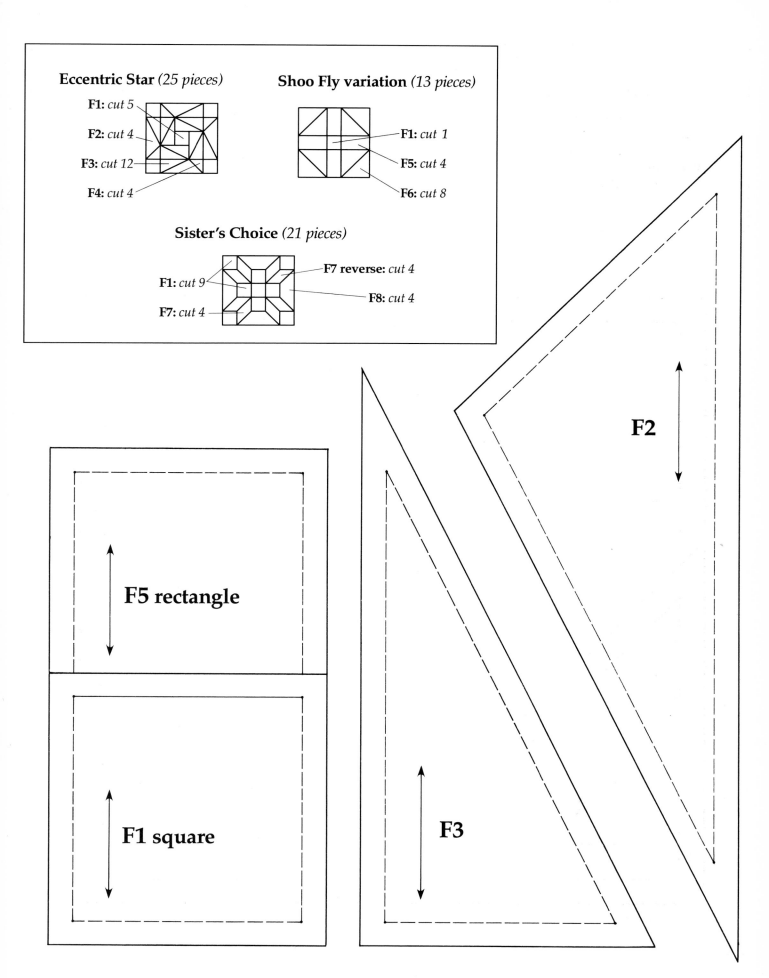

Eccentric Star *(25 pieces)*

F1: *cut 5*
F2: *cut 4*
F3: *cut 12*
F4: *cut 4*

Shoo Fly variation *(13 pieces)*

F1: *cut 1*
F5: *cut 4*
F6: *cut 8*

Sister's Choice *(21 pieces)*

F1: *cut 9*
F7 reverse: *cut 4*
F8: *cut 4*
F7: *cut 4*

F2

F5 rectangle

F1 square

F3

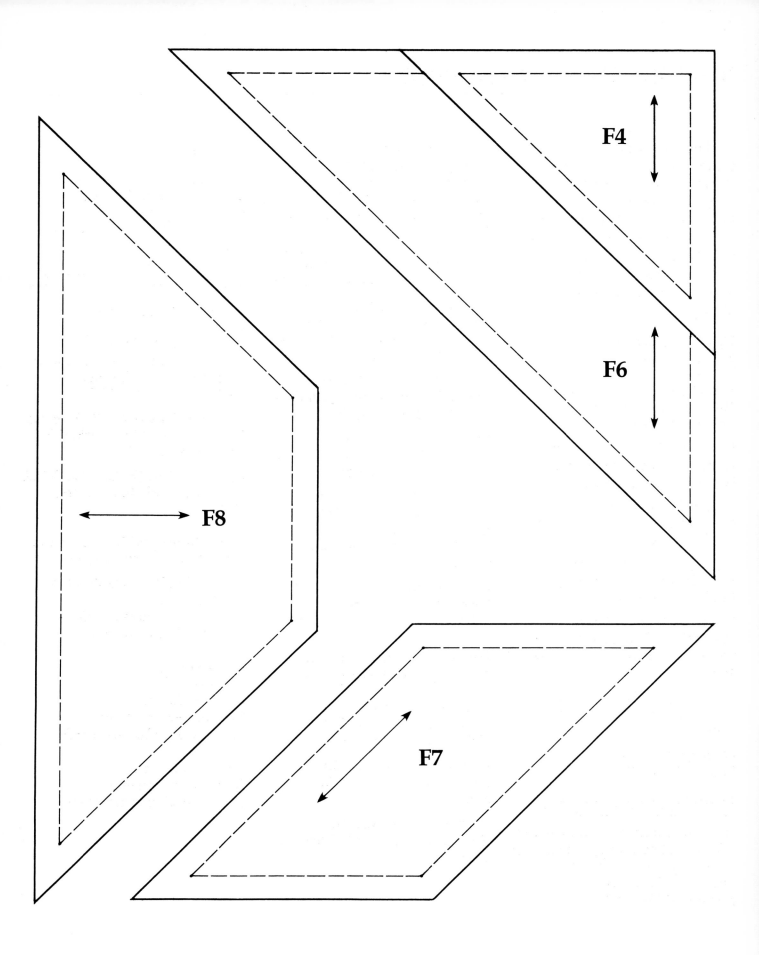

F4

F6

F8

F7

BIBLIOGRAPHY AND SUPPLIES

*T*hese books have been helpful to me as I wrote **Crosspatch**. If an * occurs, it means the title may be out of print right now. However, the * titles were good books and popular, too, so you will likely find them in a friend's quilting book stash, through your quilt guild, or at your local library.

Basic How-to on Piecing and Quilting

*Gutcheon, Beth. *The Perfect Patchwork Primer*. New York: Penguin Books, 1976.

James, Michael. *The Quiltmaker's Handbook*. Englewood Cliffs, N.J.: Prentice-Hall Inc., 1978.

Leone, Diana. *Fine Hand Quilting*. Los Altos, Calif.:Leone Publications, 1986.

_____ , *The Sampler Quilt*. Los Altos, Calif.: Leone Publications, 1980.

Puckett, Marjorie. *Patchwork Possibilities*. Orange, Calif.: Orange Patchwork Publishers, 1981.

_____ , Gail Giberson. *Primarily Patchwork*. Redlands, Calif.: Cabin Craft, 1975.

Quilting. Menlo Park, Calif.: Sunset Books, 1982.

Drafting Blocks Any Size

*French, Thomas E., and Charles J. Vierch. *A Manual of Engineering Drawing for Students and Draftsmen*. New York: McGraw-Hill, 1953.

Books With Lots of Blocks Pictured

Beyer, Jinny. *Patchwork Patterns*. McLean, Va.: EPM Publications, Inc., 1979.

_____ . *The Quilter's Album of Blocks and Borders*. McLean, Va.: EPM Publications, Inc., 1980.

Hall, Carrie, and Rose Kretsinger. *The Romance of the Patchwork Quilt in America*. New York: Dover, 1989.

*Hopkins, Mary Ellen. *The It's Okay if You Sit On My Quilt Book*. Atlanta: Yours Truly, Inc., 1982.

*Malone, Maggie. *Classic American Patchwork Quilts*. New York: Drake Publishers, 1977.

Martin, Judy. *Judy Martin's Ultimate Book of Quilt Block Patterns*. Denver: Crosley-Griffith Publishing Company, 1988.

Rehmel, Judy. *The Quilt I.D. Book*. New York: Prentice-Hall Press, 1986.

Books To Make You Think Differently About Quilts

Gutcheon, Jeffrey. *Diamond Patchwork*. Lafayette, Calif.: C & T Publishing, 1987.

Martin, Judy. *Patchworkbook*. New York: Charles Scribner's Sons, 1983.

Pasquini, Katie. *Mandala*. Eureka, Calif.: Sudz Publishing, 1983.

Dream Books

Cooper, Patricia, and Norma Bradley Buferd. *The Quilters*. Garden City, New York: Doubleday and Company, Inc., 1977.

The Esprit Quilt Collection. San Francisco: Esprit De Corp., 1985.

Lasansky, Jeanette. *Pieced by Mother, Over 100 Years of Quiltmaking Tradition*. Lewisburg, Pa.: Oral Traditions Project of Union County Historical Society, 1987.

Pottinger, David. *Quilts From the Indiana Amish*. New York: E. P. Dutton, Inc., 1983.

Rae, Janet. *The Quilts of the British Isles*. New York: E. P. Dutton, 1987.

Note: All the quilt books currently in print may be obtained from:

Quilting Books Unlimited
1158 Prairie
Aurora, Illinois 60506
Send $1.00 for catalog.

SUPPLIES

Itchin' to Stitch
34 South Walker Way
Sun Prairie, Wisconsin 53590

The Cotton Patch
1025 Brown Avenue
Lafayette, California 94549